Playing the Piano

Music Titles of Related Interest

Music Fundamentals

Leon Dallin, *Foundations in Music Theory with Programmed Exercises, 2d Edition*
William Duckworth, *Creative Approach to Music Fundamentals, 2d Edition*
Neil McKay and Marion McKay, *Fundamentals of Western Music*
Gary Martin, *Basic Concepts in Music, 2d Edition*

Skills Development

Carolynn Lindeman, *Pianolab*
Helene Robinson, *Basic Piano for Adults*
Charles Lindsley, *Fundamentals of Singing for Voice Classes*
Royal Stanton, *Steps to Singing for Voice Classes, 3d Edition*

Playing
the Piano

Phyllis Irwin

California State University
at Fresno

Wadsworth Publishing Company
Belmont, California
A Division of Wadsworth, Inc.

Music Editor: Suzanna Brabant
Editorial Assistant: Cindy Haus
Production Editor: Lisa Danchi
Print Buyer: Barbara Britton
Designer: MaryEllen Podgorski
Copy Editor: Carole Crouse
Autographer and Compositor: A-R Editions, Inc.

Printed in the United States of America   14

   3 4 5 6 7 8 9 10—92 91

Library of Congress Cataloging-in-Publication Data

Irwin, Phyllis A.
   Playing the piano.

   Includes index.
   1. Piano—Methods.   2. Piano—Methods—Group
instruction.   I. Title.
MT220.I78   1988   87–752594
ISBN 0–534-08769-8

In memory of Patricio Gutierrez

Contents

Chapter 1

A beginning   1
The piano   1
The keyboard: Exploring soft and loud—high and low   3
    Discovering the keyboard   3
    Learning about rhythm   3
    Preliminary rhythmic exercises   4
Playing black keys   4
Playing melodies   5
    Black-key exercises with fingerings   6
    Turning melodies into ensembles   9
Playing by ear   10
    Ensemble exercises   13

Chapter 2

Introduction to notation   14
    Rhythmic notation   14
Practicing rhythms   16
    Rhythmic exercises 1   16
    Pitch notation   17
Playing white keys   19
    C and F exercises   19
    Experiments with *piano* and *forte*   19
    Mezzo forte exercises   20
An intervallic approach to sight-reading   22
    Learning intervals: Seconds and thirds   22
    Learning intervals: Fourths and fifths   23
    Interval exercises   24
Theory worksheet 1   24

Chapter 3

Performing music with two hands 27
    Rhythmic exercises 2 27
Playing melodies with accompaniments 28
Understanding common time 28
Dotted notes 30
Playing melodies with both hands 35
Creating your own composition 1 36
Theory worksheet 2 37

Chapter 4

Half steps, chromatic scales, and accidentals 38
Whole steps and major scales 39
The key of F 40
    Key signatures 40
Performing rhythms containing eighth notes 42
    Rhythmic exercises 3 42
Performing music containing eighth notes 43
Theory worksheet 3 47
Creating your own composition 2 48
More music to read and play 48

Chapter 5

The key of G 50
Transposing 51
Playing in the key of G 51
    Rhythmic exercises 4 53
The pentatonic scale 54
Playing more music in the key of G 56
Increasing dexterity 57
    Technical exercise 1 57
Creating your own composition 3 58
Theory worksheet 4 59
More music to read and play 61

Chapter 6

C, F, and G chords in root position; playing triads 62
    Triad exercises 62
    Technical exercises 2 63
    More triad exercises 65
    Echo rhythms and improvisation 65
Chord progressions 66

The blues; playing a twelve-bar blues progression   66

An exercise in improvisation   67

Blue notes   67

A blues-style composition to read and play   68

Another exercise in improvisation   69

More about intervals   69

Using new blues patterns   70

Creating your own composition 4; writing a "blues"   71

Theory worksheet 5   73

Chapter 7

Studies in touch   74

Playing with different touches   75

Developing finger independence   77

    Technical exercise 3   77

    Rhythmic exercises 5   77

Moving away from five-note melodies   78

The sound of minor   81

Playing in the key of A minor   82

Creating your own composition 5   84

Theory worksheet 6   85

More music to read and play   87

Chapter 8

Playing scales   88

Key signatures   89

    Major keys   90

    Minor keys   90

    Key relationships   90

Tonic and dominant seventh chords   93

Accompaniment patterns   98

Lead sheet chord symbols   98

    Rhythmic exercises 6   99

A new time signature: $\frac{6}{8}$ 100

    Rhythmic exercises 7   100

Using the damper pedal   104

Creating your own composition 6   105

Theory worksheet 7   106

More music to read and play   107

Chapter 9

The subdominant chord   108

Playing melodies with I, IV, and V7 accompaniments   111

    Technical exercise 4   113

Syncopated rhythm   114

    Rhythmic exercises 8   114

Playing syncopated rhythms   115

    Rhythmic exercises 9   116

Lead sheet melodies   120

Creating your own composition 7; passing tones   121

Theory worksheet 8   123

More music to read and play   124

Chapter 10

A duet with syncopated rhythms   126

A new key: D minor   129

    Rhythmic exercise 10   130

    Rhythmic exercise 11   131

Performing rhythms in $\frac{2}{4}$, $\frac{3}{4}$, and $\frac{4}{4}$ with sixteenth notes   133

    Rhythmic exercises 12   134

    Technical exercise 5   135

The Dorian mode   135

Playing in the Dorian mode   136

More experiences with sixteenth notes in $\frac{2}{4}$ and $\frac{3}{4}$ 138

Creating your own composition 8   139

Theory worksheet 9   140

More music to read and play   141

Chapter 11

The key of D major   144

Playing in the key of D major   146

    Technical exercise 6   147

Playing music with more complex fingerings   150

The key of B♭ major   152

Theory worksheet 10   156

More music to read and play   157

Chapter 12

Lead sheet chord building   158
Building triads   159
Building seventh chords   160
Building sixth chords   161
A collection of popular and folk-style compositions in lead sheet arrangements   162
Theory worksheet 11   166

More advanced repertoire arranged in chronological order   168
Glossary of musical terms   187
Appendix A   188
    Lead sheet chord chart   188
Appendix B   190
    Major scales and fingerings   190
    Selected harmonic minor scales and fingerings   191
Indexes   193

Preface

Students enrolling in first-year piano classes in a college or university represent a wide range of ages, musical backgrounds, interests, and goals. Some students have absolutely no background and are in the class to fill this lack. Some students are interested in adding to whatever background they have gained in public school musical activities. Among these students with varied backgrounds, musical interests include everything from "blue grass" to jazz, from church music to "top forty," and from Bach to Bartok. Goals of the students run the gamut from learning to play some of the easier music by well-known composers to developing skills necessary for playing popular or folk music from lead sheets—or to learning to improvise their own compositions.

Playing the Piano is intended as a valuable resource to teachers and students in these group piano courses. It is designed and structured to account for all kinds of individual differences in background, physical ability, musical talent, and course goals. It springs from my years of teaching these kinds of groups at California State University at Fresno.

Approach

Because I believe that immediate and successful "hands-on" experiences are important, especially for the more insecure older students, *Playing the Piano* uses rote black-key playing activities to help students gain initial familiarity with the keyboard. In these early activities, simple black-key exercises and melodies let students play by imitation, allowing them to begin "making music" at once. Pentatonic ostinati are suggested as means of creating accompaniments for black-key melodies and providing ensemble music.

Musical notation is presented after students have had opportunities to play rote melodies. Practical keyboard exercises with rhythmic notation precede the first exercise involving both melodic and rhythmic notation. This sequence is particularly helpful for students with no musical background.

The presentation of basic musical notation is followed by simple compositions for solos and ensembles in the key of C. Five-finger melodies with and without simple accompaniments precede melodies whose ranges include notes for both hands. An intervallic approach to sight-reading is stressed and general intervals from seconds to fifths are introduced with these early melodies.

Many five-finger melodies are presented in early chapters, some of which appear in later chapters in new keys. This use of familiar materials in new keys helps students make the physical adjustments to different key signatures and their related problems (new positions on the keyboard and the playing of one or two black keys) more easily. A similar approach is used to introduce students to minor keys.

The introduction of traditional I-V7-I and I-IV-V7-I chording patterns begins in Chapter 8. However, chord symbols appear above melodic lines as early as Chapter 2. This feature, plus certain sections of the classified index ("Five-Finger Melodies," "Melodies with Two Chords," and "Melodies with Three Chords"), facilitates the use of this text by teachers who prefer to introduce five-finger melodies with chordal accompaniments earlier in the semester or the quarter.

A twelve-bar blues progression is introduced as one approach to moving out of a five-finger position. The motivational aspect of this more "popular" musical style promotes the mastery of triadic exercises based on the I, IV, and V chords. Familiarity with the chord progression provides the basis for simple improvisation by those who want to create their own music.

Theoretical information is presented only when it relates to music to be performed. The emphasis on development of playing skills is beneficial for students regardless of their musical backgrounds.

The music in the text represents as wide a variety of styles as possible in order to meet the interests and the needs of a wide range of students. Folk music contained in the book represents diverse nationalities and ethnic backgrounds. Some music is taken from the popular idiom of the twentieth century. Other music has been selected from appropriate literature by traditional eighteenth-, nineteenth, and twentieth-century composers. All the music is arranged in an order of increasing difficulty as new problems are to be mastered: an ever-expanding melodic range, new keys, and more complex rhythms to interpret. Some finger exercises are included to help students improve their technique.

Ensemble music for four hands at one piano and for two pianos is included to introduce students to the extra enjoyment that can be gained from group participation in music making.

Improvisational and compositional skills can be developed, beginning with the creation of black-key ostinati, progressing next to the creation of simple melodies on white keys, then moving to the improvising or writing of compositions based on prescribed chord progressions such as the twelve-bar blues progression included in the text. Specific creative activities are suggested throughout the book.

Rhythmic problems pose the greatest difficulties for many students in piano classes. The inclusion of numerous rhythmic exercises will help students master a wide range of rhythmic patterns.

For teachers wishing to check up on students' theoretical skills through written assignments, theory worksheets may be found at the ends of Chapters 2–12. These checkups cover everything from rhythmic and melodic notation to key signatures, scales, and chord structures.

Special features that recommend *Playing the Piano* to instructors interested in a balanced and eclectic approach to the development of keyboard skills are

1. Rote activities that ensure students' immediate involvement
2. An intervallic approach to music reading
3. Music from folk literature and eighteenth-, nineteenth, and twentieth-century composed literature for two and four hands
4. The development of improvisational skills through the creation of pentatonic ostinati in the beginning and later through the development of melodic figures based on suggested chord progressions
5. Theoretical information presented in a succinct manner only as it relates to music to be performed
6. Notes to the instructor suggesting ways to use the book
7. Introductions to new keys through familiar music
8. A guide to the building of triads and dominant seventh chords applied to lead sheet interpretation
9. The inclusion of numerous rhythmic exercises
10. The inclusion of eleven theory worksheets to check up on students' understanding of theoretical information

Chapter 1

Concepts	Skills
a beginning	playing black keys
the piano	playing melodies
the keyboard: exploring soft and loud—high and low	turning melodies into ensembles
discovering the keyboard	playing by ear
learning about rhythm	

A Beginning

Whether you are young or not so young, you can develop enough skill in this class to be able to play some of the music you enjoy. Learning to play the piano involves coordinating ear and body. For most of us, this coordination is assisted by visual input. We hear music performed; we develop an ability to remember how it sounds, and that memory helps us recreate those sounds at the piano through our manipulation of its keys. Those of us who are sighted learn to read musical notation, symbols that remind us how to recreate the sounds of music at the piano. The mind governs all these activities, taking in aural and visual stimuli, storing sounds in its memory, and controlling the physical motions necessary for playing music at the piano.

Like any new skill, the development of the ability to play the piano requires that you devote time to frequent practice so your ears, mind, eyes, and body can absorb and produce everything your teacher requires. This should be an exciting process, and one that will enable you to play music from folk literature, some jazz and popular music, and simpler compositions from the classical repertoire.

The Piano

There are several types of pianos in existence today: electronic pianos, grand pianos, upright pianos, and spinets. Although the sound-producing mechanisms inside the instruments may differ, the keyboards through which the sounds are controlled are basically the same.

The most modern development in the piano world is the electronic piano. This small and portable instrument is used in most contemporary popular music groups and is also found in many piano classrooms in which group instruction is offered. An electronic piano consists of a keyboard that controls highly sophisticated electronic equipment capable of generating and amplifying sounds.

Traditional acoustic pianos—grands, uprights, and spinets—though built today, are very similar to those in use one hundred years ago. They are composed of keyboards; sets of hammers, dampers, and strings; sounding boards; pedals; and wooden cases. The following diagram shows a grand piano, the instrument most often associated with classical concerts.

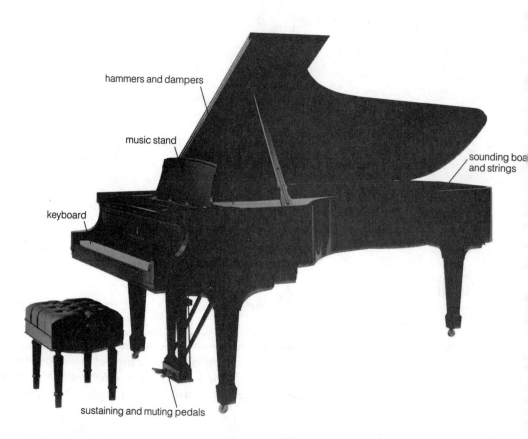

Steinway & Sons, Scale Model D concert grand. Used by permission.

Each key of the keyboard is part of a lever that, when depressed, activates a padded hammer, causing it to strike one, two, or three strings. This, in turn, produces vibrations we hear as tones. The speed and the force with which a key is depressed determine the *dynamic level* (loudness) of the tone produced. As soon as the key is released, the vibrations are stopped by a damper that settles on the string.

The Keyboard: Exploring Soft and Loud—High and Low

TO THE TEACHER: *If you prefer to begin with musical notation, please skip to Chapter 2.*

In this section you begin to make music at the piano without first learning to read notes. Through these materials and the guidance of your teacher, you will become familiar with the keyboard and learn to play some simple melodies.

Discovering the Keyboard

When playing the piano, fingers should be considered to be extensions of the arms. Weight from your back is transmitted through the arms to the hands, then to the fingers, then to the keys in order to produce tones.

1. Seat yourself in front of the middle of the keyboard.

2. Look at the arrangement of black keys. (Some are in a cluster of two keys; others are in a cluster of three keys.)

3. Make the shape shown in the illustration with each hand, allowing the fingers to curve slightly at each joint.

4. Using the index and middle fingers, depress one cluster of two black keys with each hand. (Be sure the two keys are depressed simultaneously.)

5. Using the index, middle, and ring fingers, depress one cluster of three keys with each hand. (Again, be sure all three keys are depressed simultaneously.)

6. Experiment with these clusters, making soft and loud tones by varying the speed and the force with which you depress the keys.

7. Produce long and short tones by varying the length of time you keep the keys depressed.

Learning about Rhythm

Once you have experimented with the sounds produced by clusters of black keys, you can learn to control these sounds rhythmically. *Rhythm* is a basic element of music: the organization of its sounds and silences in time. The core of rhythm in the music you will be playing consists of a steady *beat* or *pulse*, which can be loosely compared to the ticking of a clock or the beating of the human pulse.

Preliminary Rhythmic Exercises

Chant the numbers presented in the following sequences in a steady manner. Then repeat the sequences, clapping your hands once for each number you chant.

A. 1 2 1 2 1 2 1 2

B. 1 2 3 1 2 3 1 2 3 1 2 3

C. 1 2 3 4 1 2 3 4 1 2 3 4 1 2 3 4

D. 1 2 3 4 5 1 2 3 4 5 1 2 3 4 5 1 2 3 4 5

Combine these counting sequences with cluster sounds. Depress the keys of a cluster group each time an *X* appears underneath a number. Release the cluster just in time to depress it for the next *X*.

A. 1 2 1 2 1 2 1 2

    X   X   X   X

B. 1 2 3 1 2 3 1 2 3 1 2 3

    X   X   X   X

C. 1 2 3 4 1 2 3 4 1 2 3 4 1 2 3 4

    X   X   X   X

D. 1 2 3 4 5 1 2 3 4 5 1 2 3 4 5 1 2 3 4 5

    X   X   X   X

Practice these exercises with each hand separately, then with hands together. Go through each sequence with 2-key clusters, then with 3-key clusters.

Playing Black Keys

Here are some exercises requiring you to move around the keyboard, playing three clusters of black keys. The first is based on 2-key clusters.

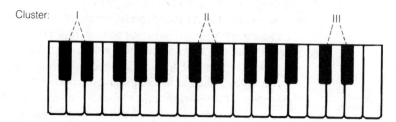

1. Count 1 2 3 4 1 2 3 4 1 2 3 4 in a slow and steady manner.

2. Play Cluster I with the left hand (L.H.), counting 1 2 3 4.
   Play Cluster II with the right hand (R.H.), counting 1 2 3 4.
   Cross the left arm over the right arm and play Cluster III with your L.H., counting 1 2 3 4.

3. Play Cluster III with the R.H., counting 1 2 3 4.
   Play Cluster II with the L.H., counting 1 2 3 4.
   Cross the right arm over the left arm and play Cluster I with your R.H., counting 1 2 3 4.

■ **TO THE STUDENT:** *Once you have become reasonably comfortable playing the 2-key clusters, be sure to move from cluster to cluster without pausing!*

Practice these procedures again, listening to the tones carefully. As you move from I to II to III, the frequencies of the vibrations you produce become more rapid, causing the pitches to sound *higher*. When you move from III to II to I, the opposite occurs. The frequencies of the vibrations you produce become less rapid, causing the pitches to sound *lower*.

The next exercise involves three 3-key clusters.

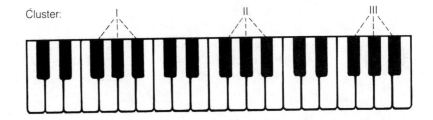

1. Count 1 2 3 4 1 2 3 4 1 2 3 4 in a slow and steady manner.

2. Play I with the L.H., counting 1 2 3 4.
   Play II with the R.H., counting 1 2 3 4.
   Cross the left arm over the right arm and play III with your L.H., counting 1 2 3 4.

3. Play III with the R.H., counting 1 2 3 4.
   Play II with the L.H., counting 1 2 3 4.
   Cross the right arm over the left arm and play I with your R.H., counting 1 2 3 4.

Playing Melodies

A *melody* is a sequence of single pitches having a beginning and an end. Melodies are played on the keyboard by depressing first one key and then another in appropriate sequences. Your fingers must be used independently to depress the keys in the proper order. If you use a typewriter or a computer, you may have developed the kind of finger independence that allows you to use those keyboards with great speed. However, at the piano the technique is quite different. The piano keys must be depressed by weighted pressure (not by pecking or tapping motions), and the transition from one key to the next must be made very smoothly. As you begin to release one key, the next must be depressed. This allows the sequence of melodic pitches to sound as *legato* (smoothly connected) as possible.

Keyboard fingering guides assign the following numbers to the five fingers on each hand.

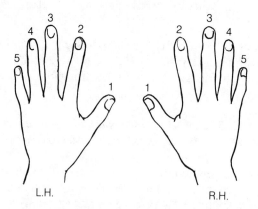

Place your hands on your lap and press each finger indicated.

A. L.H. 5–4–3–2–1

B. R.H. 1–2–3–4–5

If you were playing consecutive keys on the keyboard with each of these fingers in the order prescribed, in what direction would the pitches (sounds) move? *Up,* or *higher.* You would be playing keys in sequence from left to right.

Try the following sequence.

A. L.H. 1–2–3–4–5

B. R.H. 5–4–3–2–1

If you were playing these on the keyboard, in what direction would the pitches move? *Down,* or *lower.* You would be playing keys in sequence from right to left.

Black-Key Exercises with Fingerings

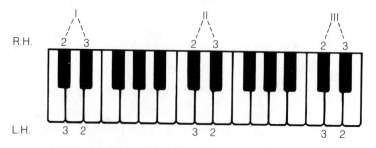

Using the same hand position indicated on page 3, with fingers curved slightly at each joint, play these exercises—one key at a time.

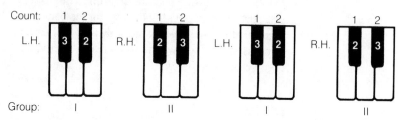

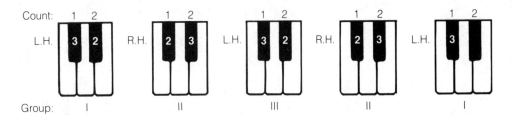

■ TO THE STUDENT: *Remember to cross the left arm over the right arm when moving from II to III.*

Here are fingerings for the 3-black-key clusters.

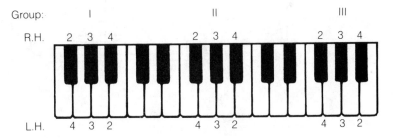

The next exercises are based on the 3-black-key clusters.

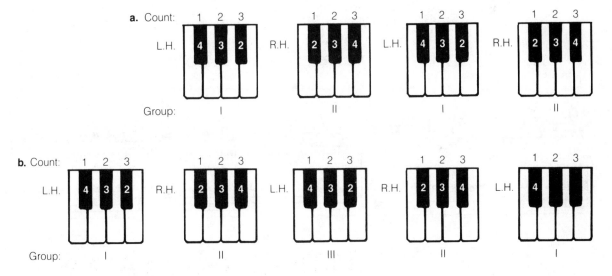

TO THE TEACHER: *The next melodies can be taught by rote or by finger number.*

The following melodies are based on pitches in the 3-key cluster of black keys. They are to be played with each hand by following the fingering guides and observing the steady beat indicated here by the symbol "I." (This mark replaces the usual counting sequence to preclude confusion between two sets of numbers.)

Steady beat: | | | | | | | | | | | | | | | |

R.H. plays: 2 3 4 – 3 2 3 – 2 3 4 2 3 4 2 –

L.H. plays: 4 3 2 – 3 4 3 – 4 3 2 4 3 2 4 –

LULLABY

Wales

Steady beat: | | | | | | | | | | | | | | | | | | | | | | | | | | | | | | | |

R.H. plays: 4 3 2 3 4 4 4 – 3 3 3 – 4 4 4 – 4 3 2 3 4 4 4 4 4 3 3 4 3 2 – – –

L.H. plays: 2 3 4 3 2 2 2 – 3 3 3 – 2 2 2 – 2 3 4 3 2 2 2 2 2 3 3 2 3 4 – – –

MERRILY WE ROLL ALONG

U.S.

In the next version of the two melodies, the two hands play simultaneously. The right hand plays the melody and the left hand plays an accompaniment, producing *harmony,* the result of two or more different pitches sounding at the same time. For greater reading ease, the beats and the melodic fingerings are grouped in fours by vertical lines.

Steady beat:	ǀ ǀ ǀ ǀ	ǀ ǀ ǀ ǀ	ǀ ǀ ǀ ǀ	ǀ ǀ ǀ ǀ
R.H. plays:	2 3 4 –	3 2 3 –	2 3 4 2	3 4 2 –
L.H. plays:	4 – – –	4 – – –	4 – – –	4 – – –

LULLABY

Wales

Steady beat:	ǀ ǀ ǀ ǀ	ǀ ǀ ǀ ǀ	ǀ ǀ ǀ ǀ	ǀ ǀ ǀ ǀ	ǀ ǀ ǀ ǀ	ǀ ǀ ǀ ǀ	ǀ ǀ ǀ ǀ	ǀ ǀ ǀ ǀ
R.H. plays:	4 3 2 3	4 4 4 –	3 3 3 –	4 4 4 –	4 3 2 3	4 4 4 4	3 3 4 3	2 – – –
L.H. plays:	4 – 4 –	4 – 4 –	4 – 4 –	4 – 4 –	4 – 4 –	4 – 4 –	4 – 4 –	4 – 4 –

MERRILY WE ROLL ALONG

U.S.

Turning Melodies into Ensembles

Folk melodies, such as the two presented here, can become the basis for ensemble music when they are accompanied by one or more simple ostinati. An *ostinato* is a short melody repeated over and over. Here are two ostinati that can be played simultaneously with "Lullaby" or "Merrily We Roll Along."

The first ostinato has been formed on a 2-key cluster:

Steady beat: | | | | | | | |
R.H.: 2 3 2 3 | 2 3 2 3
L.H.: 3 2 3 2 | 3 2 3 2   etc.

The second ostinato is based on a 3-key cluster:

Steady beat: | | | | | | | |
R.H.: 4 2 4 2 | 4 2 4 2
L.H.: 2 4 2 4 | 2 4 2 4   etc.

You may want to create your own ostinati. Any sequence of black keys can be used as long as it fits the tempo (the speed) of the beat established by the teacher or by another player—or by you. You can also create ensemble music by playing your ostinato together with ostinati played by one or more of your colleagues.

Playing by Ear

The ability to play music "by ear"—that is, by simply imitating at the piano (or on another instrument) a melody or a composition you have heard—can be a wonderful source of musical enjoyment. The development of this skill requires careful listening, both to the pitches of the music you wish to reproduce and to the pitches of the keys you play on the piano.

A number of melodies can be played on the black keys of the piano. They usually involve playing keys of two or more adjacent clusters (both 2- and 3-key clusters). If you are familiar with some of the folk songs listed here, try to pick out their melodies on the keyboard. A guide to the necessary keys is given, and an arrow indicates the key that will produce the first pitch of the melody.

TO THE TEACHER: *The melodies are notated for your assistance.*

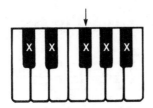

OLD MACDONALD

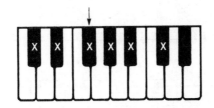

MAMA DON'T 'LOW

AMAZING GRACE

AULD LANG SYNE

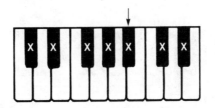

SWING LOW, SWEET CHARIOT

Ensemble Exercises

The ostinati on the previous pages can be used to accompany melodies 1, 2, 4, and 5.

Chapter 2

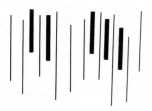

Concepts	Skills
introduction to notation	practicing rhythms
rhythmic notation	playing white keys
pitch notation	
an intervallic approach to sight-reading	
learning intervals: second and thirds	
learning intervals: fourths and fifths	

Introduction to Notation

Musical notation involves symbols for both rhythm and pitch. Developing an ability to interpret this notation is a necessary part of learning to play the piano. This music-reading skill can be developed easily by giving careful attention to the information presented in this book and to the guidance of your teacher.

Rhythmic Notation

The rhythmic element of music consists of three ingredients: *beat* (with which you have already dealt); groupings of beats, called *meter;* and *patterns,* composed of sounds and silences of varying lengths. The *meter* of music—the number of beats grouped together—is indicated by the top figure in each *time signature* ($\frac{2}{4}$ $\frac{3}{4}$ $\frac{4}{4}$ $\frac{6}{8}$ $\frac{3}{8}$). *Bar lines* (the vertical lines that intersect a *staff*   ) are used to separate each metrical group into a *measure. Notes* (o, ♩, ♪), which are the symbols for sounds, and *rests* ( ), or symbols for silences, combine to form *rhythmic patterns.*

To understand rhythm and its notation better, take a closer look at the musical symbols and their values. Notes and rests, the symbols for sounds and silences, have mathematical relationships.

NOTES   RESPECTS

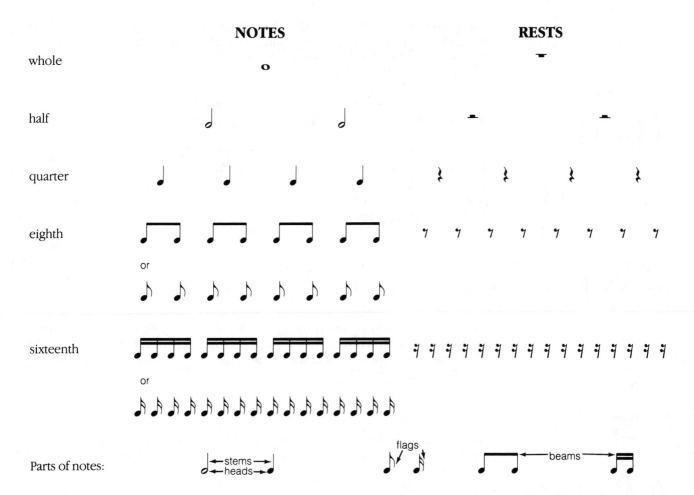

whole

half

quarter

eighth

or

sixteenth

or

Parts of notes:

Each symbol represents a relative time value, as indicated in the following graph:

Time signatures designate the meter and assign note and rest values in musical notation. The upper number in a time signature indicates the number of beats grouped together in each measure marked by bar lines in the music. The lower number represents the kind of note equivalent to one beat.

2 = 2 beats per measure
4 = ♩ equals one beat

3 = 3 beats per measure
4 = ♩ equals one beat

4 = 4 beats per measure
4 = ♩ equals one beats

2 = 2 beats per measure
2 = ♩ equals one beat

6 = 6 beats per measure
8 = ♪ equals one beat

Practicing Rhythms

There are at least two ways to practice each of the following rhythmic patterns. First, chant the counts for the beats in each measure and clap once for each note at the appropriate time. Second, chant the counts again, but this time play a note from a black-key cluster for each note.

Rhythmic Exercises 1

TO THE TEACHER: *These rhythmic patterns can also be used for rote echo clapping or echo playing as warm-up activities prior to the actual reading exercise. If you have the interest and the space, have students clap the patterns while stepping the beat.*

Count: 1 2   1 2   1 2   1 2

Count: 1 2 3   1 2 3   1 2 3   1 2 3

Pitch Notation

Notes are placed on five horizontal lines and four spaces forming a *staff*.

Notes whose heads are placed in this manner indicate a series of pitches moving upward.

Notes whose heads are placed in this manner indicate a series of pitches moving downward.

Precise pitches are assigned to the lines and spaces of each staff by a *clef*.

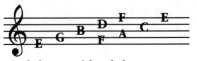

G clef, or treble clef

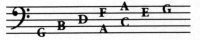

F clef, or bass clef

Piano music is generally written on a *grand staff,* two staffs joined together, on which the pitches on the upper staff are assigned by the *G clef,* or *treble clef,* and the pitches on the lower staff are assigned by the *F* or *bass clef.* Normally the right hand plays notes written on the top staff and the left hand plays notes written on the bottom staff.

Pitch names are the first seven letters of the alphabet: A–B–C–D–E–F–G. The following diagram indicates the letter names assigned to the lines and spaces of the grand staff and relates them to the white keys of the keyboard bearing the corresponding names.

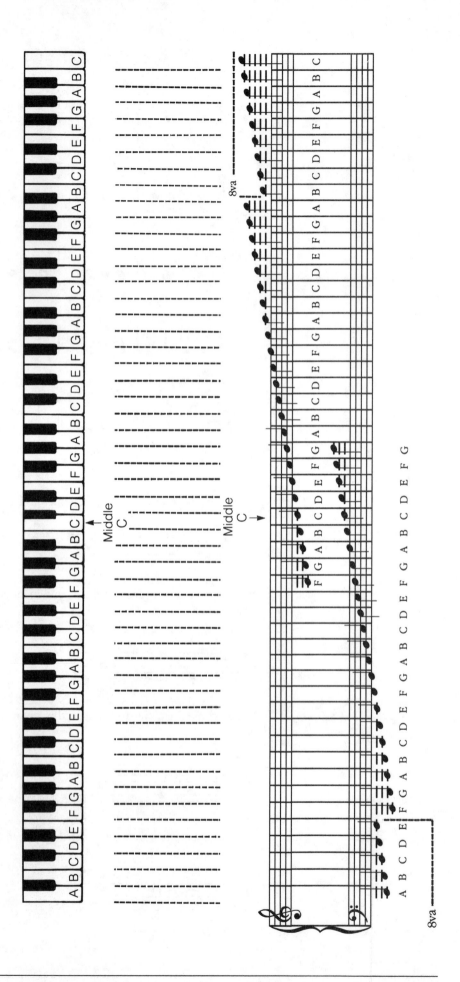

Notice that *ledger* lines and spaces can be added below and above each staff. Here are those that you will find most often in this book.

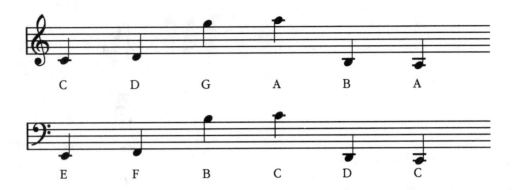

Playing White Keys

The black-key groups with which you have become familiar can serve as landmarks or guides that will help you find your way around the white keys on the keyboard. The following illustration of part of a keyboard shows the arrangement of both black and white keys, identifying the white keys by their letter names. Notice the placement of C and F.

C and F Exercises

1. Play all the Cs on the keyboard, counting 1–2–3–4 for each C. Use either one hand or both hands and any fingering.

2. Play all the Fs on the keyboard, counting 1–2–3–4 for each F. Use either one hand or both hands and any fingering.

Experiments with *Piano* and *Forte*

1. Place your right hand over the keyboard with fingers lightly touching keys in this order:

Experiment with the amount of energy or force needed to play each of the five keys both *f* (symbol for the Italian term *forte* [fór-tay], meaning loud) and *p* (symbol for the Italian term *piano* [pe-áh-no], meaning soft).

2. Place your left hand over the keyboard with fingers lightly touching the keys in this order:

Play each of the five keys both *forte* and *piano* with the left hand.

Mezzo Forte Exercises

1. Play each key four times with the R.H. fingers assigned, counting steadily 1–2–3–4–1–2–3–4, and so on. Use the amount of energy or force needed to play each note *mf* (symbol for the Italian term *mezzo forte* [mét-so fór-tay], meaning medium loud).

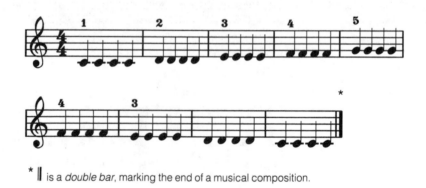

* ‖ is a *double bar*, marking the end of a musical composition.

2. Repeat the exercise with the L.H. fingers assigned.

■ **TO THE STUDENT:** *Play these folk melodies, first with the right hand and then with the left.*

TO THE TEACHER: *These melodies could be played using the finger numbers.*

JINGLE BELLS

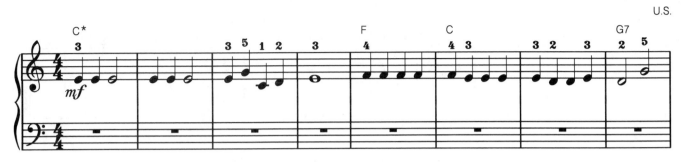

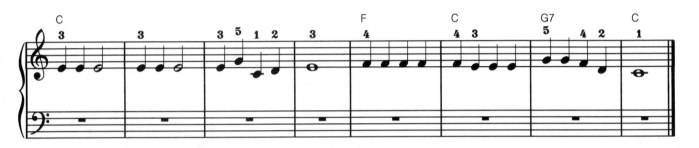

*Chord symbols can be used to create harmonic accompaniments later on.

JINGLE BELLS

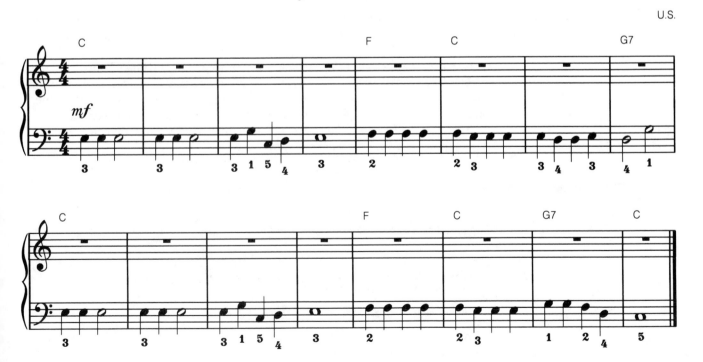

MELODY

Germany

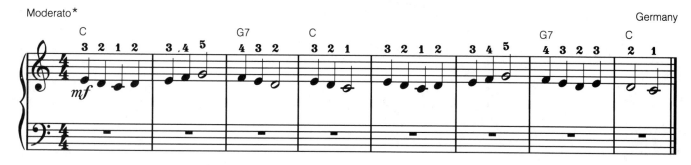

Moderato is a tempo marking indicating a moderate speed.

MELODY

Moderato

Germany

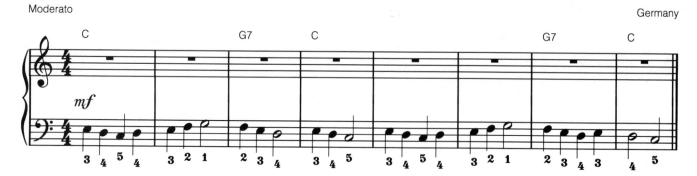

An Intervallic Approach to Sight-Reading

Sight-reading, the art of playing a piece of music the first time you read its notation, can be developed most quickly if you become familiar with *intervals* (musical distances), their notation, and their feel at the piano. First, your eyes must learn to recognize intervals from their appearance in notation. Next, your hands and fingers must learn the feel of the keyboard distances that form each of the intervals. When these reactions to notation eventually become automatic, sight-reading becomes an enjoyable, spontaneous experience rather than the laborious chore it often is at the beginning.

This section presents an introduction to the melodic intervals you will encounter frequently in the music you will be playing.

Learning Intervals: Seconds and Thirds

When notes move from a line to the next space

or from a space to the next line

you move from one key to the adjacent key in the appropriate direction. These intervals are called *seconds.*

When notes move from a line to the next line

or from a space to the next space

you move from one key to the second key away in the appropriate direction. These intervals are called *thirds.*

22

The following pieces contain several examples of these two melodic intervals: seconds and thirds.

LIGHTLY ROW

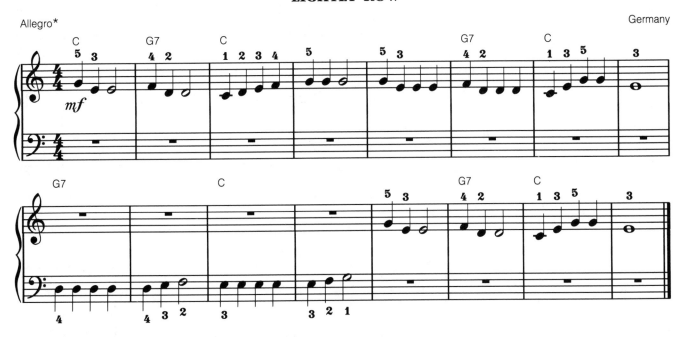

Allegro is a tempo marking indicating a lively speed.

CATCH

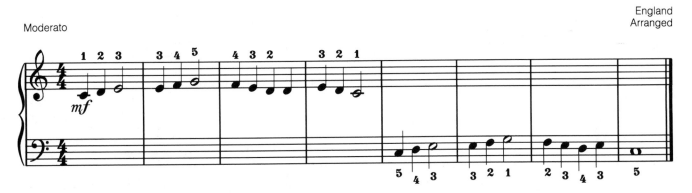

Learning Intervals: Fourths and Fifths

Sometimes notes move from a line to the second space away

or from a space to the second line away .

These intervals are called *fourths.* When you play fourths, you move from one key to the third key away in the appropriate direction.

Sometimes notes move from a space to the second space away

or from a line to the second line away

These intervals are called *fifths.* When you play fifths, you move from one key to the fourth key away in the appropriate direction.

Interval Exercises

These exercises will help you become more familiar with fourths and fifths. Play them several times, first slowly, and then try playing them at a quicker pace without pausing.

MOSTLY FOURTHS

MOSTLY FIFTHS

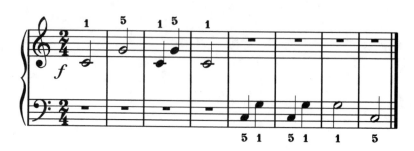

Theory Worksheet 1

A. Complete these equations by adding a note or a rest.

1. ♩ = ♪ +

2. ♪ = ♬ +

3. o = ♩ +

4. ♩ = ♫ +

5. ♩ = ♩ +

6. ▬ = ▬ +

7. 𝄽 = 𝄾 +

8. ▬ = 𝄽 +

9. 𝄽 = 𝄾 𝄾 +

10. 𝄾 = 𝄾 +

B. Above each note or rest write the number of counts it receives.

1.

2.

3.

C. Create four measures of rhythmic notation for each time signature.

1. **2/4**

2. **3/4**

3. **4/4**

D. Write the letter name of each pitch indicated beneath the notes.

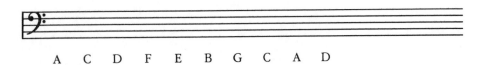

E. Place a whole note on a line or space whose pitch name corresponds to the letter given.

A   C   D   F   E   B   G   C   A   D

F. 1. _____ is the organization of musical sounds in time.

2. A _____ is a sequence of single pitches having a beginning and an end.

3. _____ results from sounding two or more different pitches at the same time.

4. An _____ is a short melody repeated over and over.

5. The steady pulse in music is called the _____.

6. Notes are placed on horizontal lines and spaces called a

_____.

7. Pitches are assigned to the lines and spaces by a _____.

G. Identify each of these ten intervals as a 2nd, a 3rd, a 4th, or a 5th.

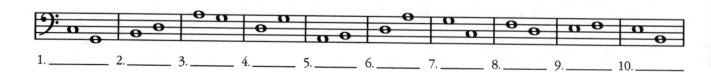

1. _____ 2. _____ 3. _____ 4. _____ 5. _____ 6. _____ 7. _____ 8. _____ 9. _____ 10. _____

Chapter 3

Concepts	Skills
understanding common time	performing music with two hands
dotted notes	playing melodies with accompaniments
	playing melodies with both hands

Performing Music with Two Hands

In this chapter you will begin to read and play music with your left and right hands simultaneously. "Rhythmic Exercises 2" will prepare you for the music that follows.

Rhythmic Exercises 2

The following exercises can be tapped while counting.

Playing Melodies with Accompaniments

■ **TO THE STUDENT:** *Play these melodies slowly and steadily at first, concentrating on both hands at once. Be sure your eyes move ahead of your playing.*

MELODY

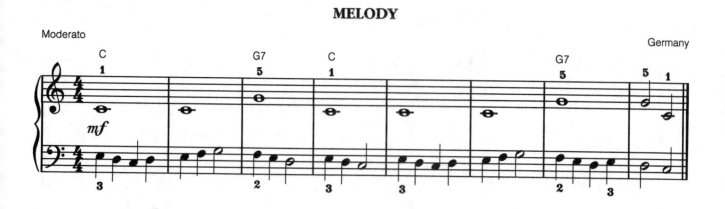

Understanding Common Time

The new time signature appearing in this next piece, C, means the same thing as the signature $\frac{4}{4}$. This time signature is referred to as *common time*.

THE BEE

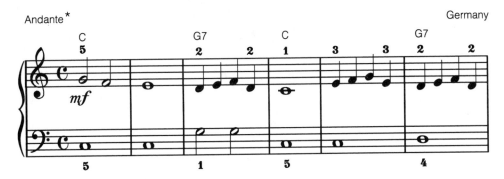

Andante is a tempo marking indicating a "walking" speed.

THE BEE

Dotted Notes

Adding a dot to a note increases its value by 1/2.

WESTMINSTER CHIMES

Andante   England

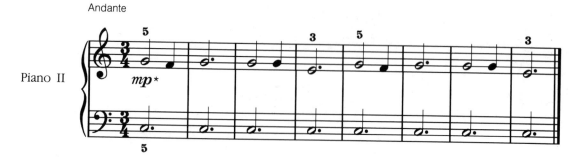

Here is a second piano part for ensemble playing.

Andante

Piano II

* **mp** is the abbreviation for the Italian term *mezzo piano*, indicating that the dynamic level should be medium soft.

A New Position for the Left Hand

OLD MACDONALD

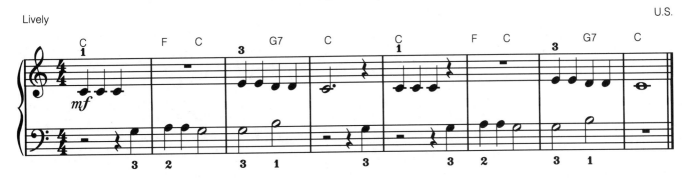

Now try this familiar piece with accompaniment and second piano part.

JINGLE BELLS

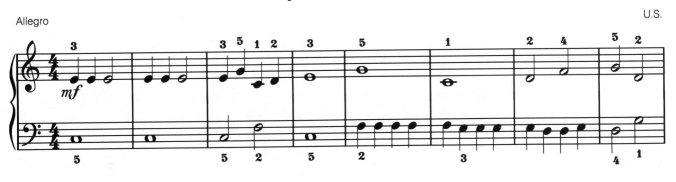

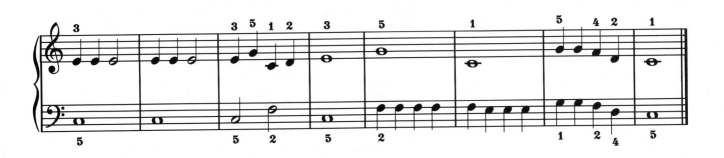

Another Left-Hand Position:

Right-Hand Position:

Allegro

Piano II

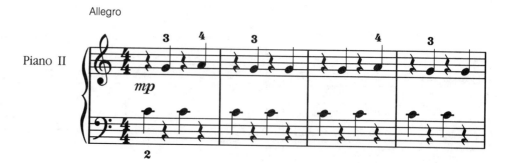

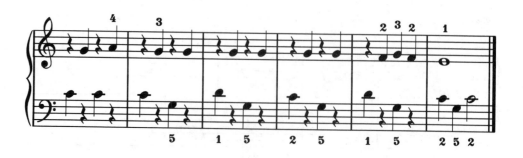

■ **TO THE STUDENT:** *Here are some more pieces you will enjoy playing with both hands. Always remember to figure out the appropriate hand positions before you play each new composition.*

New Positions for Both Hands

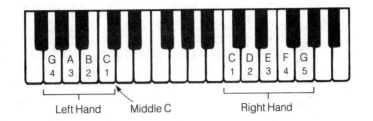

Left Hand   Middle C   Right Hand

AT THE BEGINNING

Moderato

David Gottlob Türk (1756–1813)

ODE TO JOY
(Symphony No. 9)

Ludwig van Beethoven (1770–1827)
Arranged P.I.

Allegro

THEME
(Symphony No. 2)

Johannes Brahms (1833–1897)
Arranged

Andante

CATCH AS CATCH CANON

Moderato

England

MY DOVE

Czechoslovakia

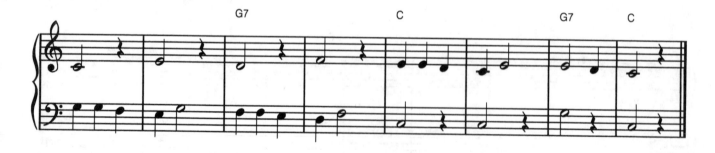

MARCH

Finland

Playing Melodies with Both Hands

When the left and right hands play a melody simultaneously, the fingering for the left hand is the opposite of that for the right hand.

Here are two folk melodies to be played with your right and left hands together.

THE CUCKOO

MANDANDIRAN

Allegro

Chile

Creating Your Own Composition 1

The following eight-measure rhythm in $\frac{4}{4}$ is suggested as a means of helping you create your own composition. You can make your own melody by assigning one of these four pitches, C–D–E–G, to each note in these eight measures. The final note should be C in order to make the piece sound finished. You may write the letter names of the pitches you choose above the notes so you can play it as often as you wish.

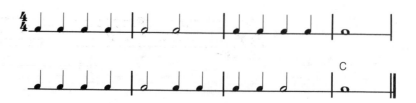

The following ostinato can be played with your left hand to provide a suitable accompaniment.

Theory Worksheet 2

A. Complete each measure by adding two notes or two rests.

B. Fill in the blanks.
1. *f (forte)* indicates a _____ dynamic level.

2. The term _____ refers to the speed of the beat.

3. *p (piano)* indicates a _____ dynamic level.

4. *Moderato* indicates a _____ speed.

5. A lively speed is indicated by the marking _____.

6. *mf (mezzo forte)* indicates a _____ dynamic level.

7. *Andante* indicates a _____ speed.

8. Common time (**C**) is the same as _____.

9. *mp (mezzo piano)* indicates a _____ dynamic level.

C. Write the letter name of each pitch below the staff.

Chapter 4

Concepts	Skills
half steps, chromatic scales, and accidentals	performing rhythms containing eighth notes
whole steps and major scales	performing music containing eighth notes
the key of f	
key signatures	

Half Steps, Chromatic Scales, and Accidentals

The smallest musical interval (distance) represented by keys on the piano is the *half step,* the distance from one key to the very next key.

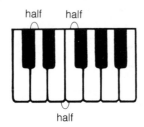

Without worrying about fingering, play all the keys (black and white) from one C up to the next. When you play a series of half steps like this, you are playing a *chromatic scale.*

The *flat sign* (♭) in music indicates that a note is to be sounded one half step lower than usual. Each black key has a flat name derived from the white key to its immediate right. Here are all the flats depicted on the keyboard. (Notice that F♭ and C♭ are white keys.)

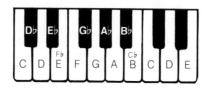

The *sharp sign* (♯) in music indicates that a note is to be sounded one half step higher than usual. Each black key has a sharp name derived from the white key to its immediate left. Here are all the sharps depicted on the keyboard. (Notice that B♯ and E♯ are white keys.)

So, each key has two names. For instance, the first of the two black keys together is called both D♭ and C♯. These two names are referred to as *enharmonic equivalents*. Play your chromatic scale once more and recite the enharmonic equivalent names for each pitch. If you have trouble doing this, look back at the preceding two diagrams.

When sharp or flat pitches are referred to by letter names, the letter name is presented first and the ♯ or the ♭ follows. On the staff, the ♯ or the ♭ precedes the note to be raised or lowered. When ♯s or ♭s are placed directly in front of notes to be affected, they are called *accidentals*.

Whole Steps and Major Scales

An interval containing two half steps is called a *whole step*.

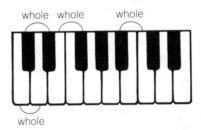

When you play each white key in order from one C up to the next, you find that some of the intervals are whole steps and some are half steps. The music you have played from the beginning of Chapter 2 has involved pitches produced on the keyboard by white keys only. All the music has been in the *key of C;* that is, the pitches belong to the series known as the *C major scale*.

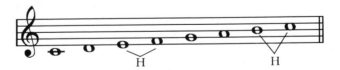

The C major scale is a series of eight pitches beginning and ending on C. Notice that the intervals between the third and fourth and the seventh and eighth pitches in the scale are half steps. All the other intervals are larger. They are whole steps.

The next compositions involve the use of a black key, B♭, and are in the *key of F*. That is, their pitches belong to the series known as the *F major scale*.

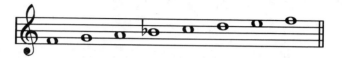

If you analyze the intervals in the F major scale, you will notice that they follow the same order of whole steps and half steps found in the C major scale: whole, whole, half, whole, whole, whole, half. This arrangement of steps always produces the series of pitches referred to as a *major scale*.

New Hand Positions

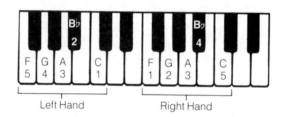

Left Hand   Right Hand

ODE TO JOY

Allegro

Ludwig van Beethoven
Arranged

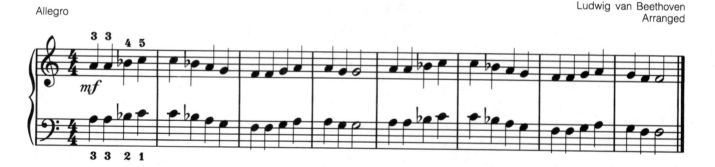

mf

Key Signatures

A *key signature* follows the clef sign on each staff of every musical composition and indicates the key, or scale sequence, to which the pitches belong. Music in the key of C requires nothing to appear after the clef sign. Music in the key of F requires the placement of a ♭ on a single line representing the pitch B, indicating that all Bs are to be performed as B-flat.

JINGLE BELLS

Allegro

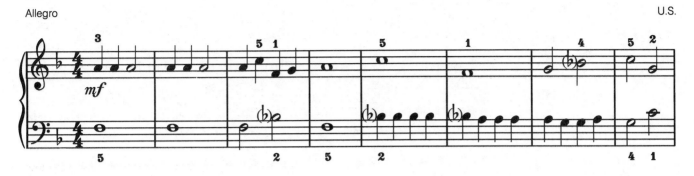

Frequently a composition begins with an incomplete measure, a measure containing fewer notes and/or rests than are necessary according to the time signature. In these instances, the final measure is also incomplete, containing the notes or rests needed to complete the first measure. Notice that the next composition begins and ends with just such incomplete measures.

WHEN THE SAINTS GO MARCHING IN

U.S.

Lively

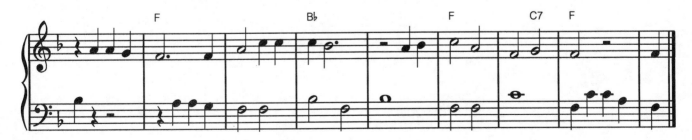

Performing Rhythms Containing Eighth Notes

Rhythmic Exercises 3

The following exercises are to be clapped, tapped, or played to prepare you for compositions in $\frac{4}{4}$ and $\frac{3}{4}$ that include eighth notes.

■ **TO THE STUDENT:** *Adding the word* and *after every numerical count to represent the second half of each beat will help you place each eighth note correctly.*

TO THE TEACHER: *These exercises can be used for echo clapping or echo playing as well as for reading.*

1.   Count: 1 & 2 & 3 & 4 &   1 & 2 & 3 & 4 &

2.   Count: 1 & 2 & 3 &   1 & 2 & 3 &

Ensemble music can be *improvised* (made up on the spot) by creating and combining black-key ostinati based on one or two measures of the rhythms in Exercise 1 or Exercise 2.

The following exercises are for two hands and are to be tapped or played.

1. Count: 1 & 2 & 3 & 4 &   1 & 2 & 3 & 4 &

2. Count: 1 & 2 & 3 &   1 & 2 & 3 &

3. Count: 1 & 2 & 3 &   1 & 2 & 3 &

Performing Music Containing Eighth Notes

QUICKER, QUICKER! ROUND AND ROUND

Allegro

David Gottlob Türk

TURKEY IN THE STRAW

Allegro

U.S.

A New Left-Hand Position

Try the following ensemble piece for more practice in the key of F.

FOLK DANCE

Allegro

France

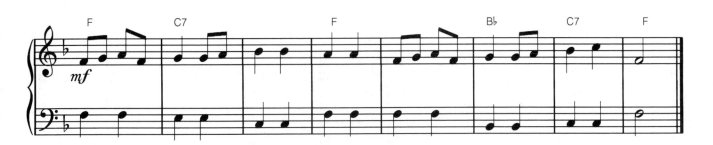

THREE SONS

Moderato

U.S.

*A *tie* is a curved line connecting two notes with the same pitch. The first note is played and sustained for the total time value of both notes.

LOVE SOMEBODY

Lively

Theory Worksheet 3

A. In each of the following series there are enough notes and rests to fill five measures. Add bar lines to indicate the ends of the measures.

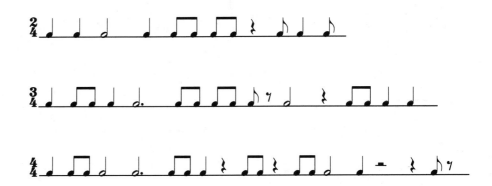

B. In the blanks provided, identify the following intervals as half steps or whole steps.

___ ___ ___ ___ ___ ___ ___

C. Write the pattern of steps that makes a major scale, using *W* for whole steps and *H* for half steps.

1. _____ 2. _____ 3. _____ 4. _____ 5. _____ 6. _____ 7. _____

D. Fill in the blanks.

1. F♯ and G♭ can be referred to as _____.

2. A flat is a musical symbol indicating that a pitch is to be _____ a half step.

3. A sharp is a musical symbol indicating that a pitch is to be _____ a half step.

4. A _____ is a curved line connecting two notes with the same pitch.

5. A sharp or a flat placed directly in front of a note in a composition is called an

_____.

Creating Your Own Composition 2

Select rhythms from the following measures and arrange them in an order of your choice to create eight measures in $\frac{3}{4}$ time. Write them in the space provided.

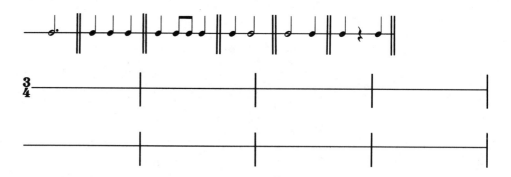

Assign one of the pitches F, G, A, and C to each note as you did in the similar assignment in Chapter 3. The use of F for the final note will make the melody sound more finished. Practice your melody several times. When you can play it successfully, add the following suggested ostinato for a left-hand accompaniment.

etc.

More Music to Read and Play

SHEPHERD'S HEY

Allegro

England

FOLK DANCE

Moderato

Poland
Arranged

MY LORD! WHAT A MORNING

U.S.

Chapter 5

Concepts	Skills
the key of g	playing in the key of g
transposing	increasing dexterity
the pentatonic scale	

The Key of G

The next compositions are in the *key of G*. Their pitches belong to the series called the *G major scale*.

New Hand Positions

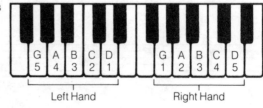

LIGHTLY ROW

Germany

Transposing

Sometimes it is convenient for a melody or composition to be played or written in a key or at a pitch level different from that of the original. Making these changes is referred to as *transposing*. You played the next pieces in the key of F in Chapter 4. Here, they are *transposed* to the key of G.

Playing in the Key of G

Pieces in the key of G will always have one sharp: F♯. Try out these songs—some familiar, some not so familiar—and see how well you do.

JINGLE BELLS

U.S.

Allegro

WHEN THE SAINTS GO MARCHING IN

Lively

U.S.

IN THE VINEYARD

Moderato

Traditional

52

Another Left-Hand Position

CHRISTMAS SONG

Allegro

Germany

Rhythmic Exercises 4

These exercises are to be tapped or rapped with each hand separately, then with hands together.

Count: 1 2   1 2   1 2   1 2

The Pentatonic Scale

Some music is based on a *pentatonic (five-toned) scale*. All the melodies and ostinati suggested in Chapter 1 are based on the pentatonic scale formed by the five black keys on the keyboard: F♯ (G♭), G♯ (A♭), A♯ (B♭), C♯ (D♭), and D♯ (E♭). F♯ (or G♭) is the first pitch in that pentatonic scale. The following duet, based on a Chinese folk melody, utilizes the pentatonic scale in which G is the first pitch. The duet also utilizes the key signature representing G major.

These are the hand positions required in "Feng Yang."

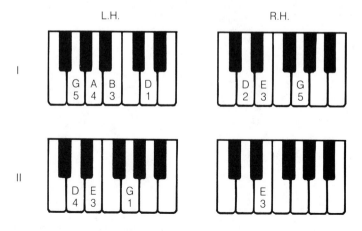

FENG YANG

Moderato

China

TO THE TEACHER: *Students could transpose these five-finger pieces to the keys of F and C.*

DANCE

Allegro

Mexico

DU, DU LIEGST MIR IM HERZEN

Moderato

Germany

The following exercise will help you develop speed and independence of fingers. First, practice it slowly with each hand alone. Maintain a good hand position, taking particular care that the fourth and fifth fingers are not allowed to flatten out. When you can play the exercise easily with separate hands, practice hands together, gradually increasing your speed. Notice that there is a two-measure melodic pattern that is repeated, beginning each time on the next white key to the right.

Technical Exercise 1

In the following ensemble piece the parts for the two pianos are joined together.

■ **TO THE STUDENT:** *Be sure to locate your own part on the staves before playing!*

FAIS DO DO

Moderato

France

Creating Your Own Composition 3

First, create eight measures of rhythm in $\frac{2}{4}$ time, limiting yourself to these symbols: ♩, ♪, ♫, ♩ . Next, assign pitches to each note, selected from G, A, B, and D. (Using G as the final pitch will make your melody sound finished.) Write your melody with its rhythmic notation on the treble staff of the grand staff provided here.

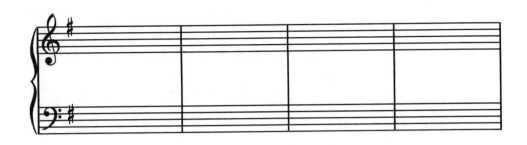

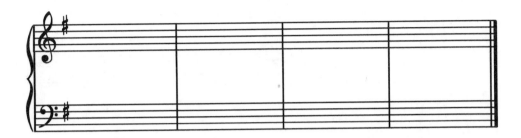

Add an accompaniment chosen from the following ostinati and notate it on the bass staff below your melody. Practice your composition until you can play it smoothly. Play it for your classmates; then invite one of your classmates to play your piece.

Theory Worksheet 4

A. Write the appropriate counting procedures above the notes in the following rhythm examples.

Count:

Count:

Count:

B. Complete the major scales indicated.

G major

F major

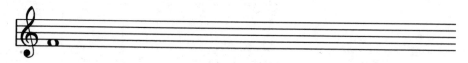

C. Write the letter note of each pitch below the staff.

_ _ _ _ _ _ _ _ _ _ _ _ _ _

_ _ _ _ _ _ _ _ _ _ _ _ _ _

D. Add a whole note to the right of each note given to form the interval indicated below the staff.

     2nd   4th   5th   3rd

More Music to Read and Play

■ **TO THE STUDENT:** *Be sure to check key signature and hand position before beginning!*

GO FROM MY WINDOW

Andante

England

MINUET IN C

Georg Friedrich Händel (1685–1759)
Arranged

Moderato

Chapter 6

Concepts	Skills
c, f, and g chords in root position	playing triads
chord progressions	playing a twelve-bar blues progression
the blues	exercises in improvisation
blue notes	using new blue patterns
more about intervals	writing a "blues"

C, F, and G Chords in Root Position; Playing Triads

Play the keys C, E, and G singly. Then play all three at the same time. Do this first with the left hand, then with the right hand.

■ **TO THE STUDENT:** *Be sure your weight is transferred through the appropriate fingers to the keys at the same time in order to sound the pitches simultaneously.*

You have just played a *triad* (a three-toned chord). This triad, whose three tones are C, E, and G, can be called a *C chord* because its lowest tone (its root) is C.

Triad Exercises

1. Play the following sequence, one key at a time, alternating hands. Move from low to high. Your eyes should focus on the next position of the chord on the keyboard as you move from one chord to the next.

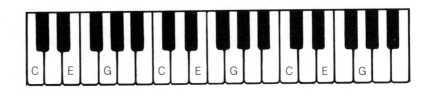

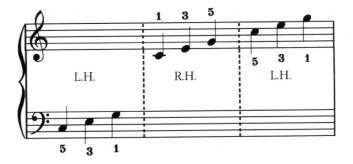

2. Play the sequence in reverse order.

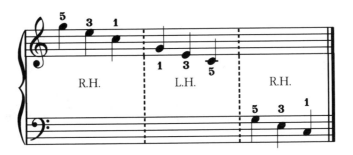

Technical Exercises 2

The following exercises will help you master the art of playing all three notes in a triad simultaneously. Practice them slowly.

■ **TO THE STUDENT:** *Be sure that each hand maintains a good position. Don't let it flatten out toward the fourth and fifth fingers!*

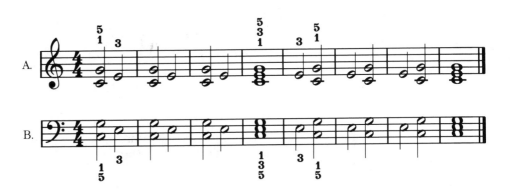

Here are two more triads to learn: the *F chord* and the *G chord*.

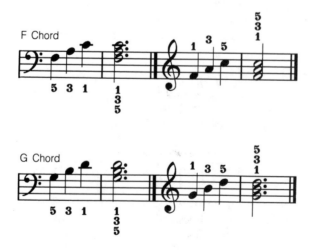

More Triad Exercises

1.

2.

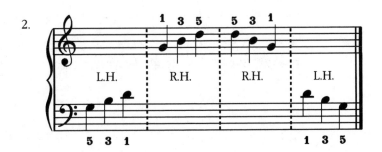

Echo Rhythms and Improvisation

1. Your instructor will clap or tap each of the following patterns and ask you to echo it.

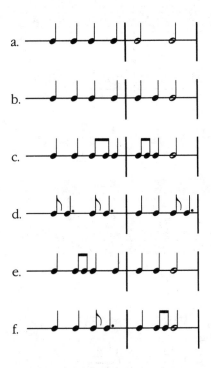

2. Your instructor will clap or tap these same rhythmic patterns and invite you to improvise echoes on your keyboard. Your echoes should be based on one, two, or all three pitches from the C chord and played with one hand alone.

3.   Repeat Exercise 2 using tones from the F chord.

4.   Repeat Exercise 2 using tones from the G chord.

Chord Progressions

A *chord progression* is a series of chords played one at a time. Practice the following chord progressions slowly, one hand at a time, until you can make the transition from one triad to another without great difficulty; then practice them with hands together.

■ **TO THE STUDENT:** *Locate the lowest key in each new triad with your eyes before moving your hand to the next position.*

TRIADS TO TRY

P.I.

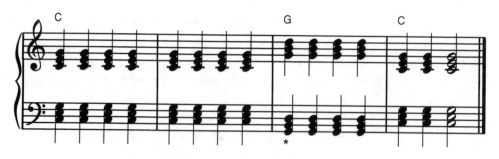

*Watch out! A new position!

The Blues; Playing a Twelve-Bar Blues Progression

The blues are distinctly American music that originated as a part of Black musical tradition in the United States. The next chord progression is one characteristic of the American "blues" heritage. Play it slowly, first one hand at a time, then hands together. Observe the accent marks (>) indicating that the notes on the second and fourth beats of each measure are to be played with greater emphasis. (Normally the first and third beats would be emphasized in $\frac{4}{4}$. The stressing of the second and fourth beats creates *syncopation,* another characteristic of blues.)

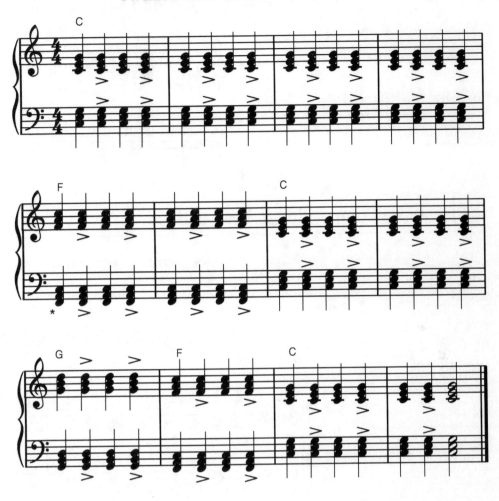

*Another new position to read!

An Exercise in Improvisation

Once you can play the twelve-bar blues progression without difficulty, play the triads as written with one hand and, with the other hand, improvise a melody based on the three tones of the appropriate triad for each measure.

TO THE TEACHER: *You may want to demonstrate this procedure to the class.*

Blue Notes

Another characteristic of the blues style is the frequent use of lowered notes called *blue notes*. The first blue notes you are going to learn are those produced by lowering the middle note of each of the three triads you have been using. Names are assigned to the three notes in a triad as follows:

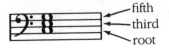

The top two notes have names referring to their distances from the lowest note, the *root*.
Your first blue notes are lowered, or flatted, thirds.

Blue notes

Triads

A Blues-Style Composition to Read and Play

In "Blue Note Blues," you will see a new musical sign: ♮ is a *natural sign.* It cancels a flat or a sharp for an entire measure.

Notice that the right and left hands shift positions simultaneously.

BLUE NOTE BLUES

Andante

P.A.I.

Another Exercise in Improvisation

Play the triads of the twelve-bar blues progression with one hand, and, with the other hand, improvise a melody based on the three tones of each triad *plus* the blue note you have learned.

More about Intervals

You have already become familiar with a few musical intervals: seconds, thirds, fourths, and fifths. Here is a guide to those and other intervals, showing how the name of each interval is derived from the number of staff degrees (lines and spaces) included in the distance. *Notice that the counting always begins with the line or the space of the first note.*

prime   2nd   3rd   4th   5th   6th   7th   octave
or   8va
unison

Intervals can be *melodic* (with the tones sounding consecutively) or *harmonic* (with the tones sounding simultaneously). Before you play the following exercises, analyze the intervals carefully. What intervals do you find? Are they melodic or harmonic? What fingerings are you to use?

Practice each hand separately, then try hands together.

Using New Blues Patterns

Here are two new patterns for you to use with your twelve-bar blues chord progression. One of these patterns incorporates the interval of a sixth.

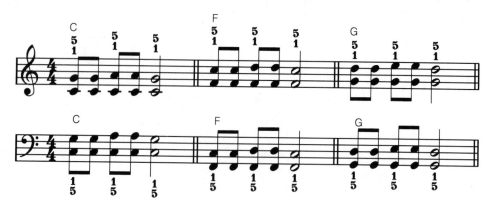

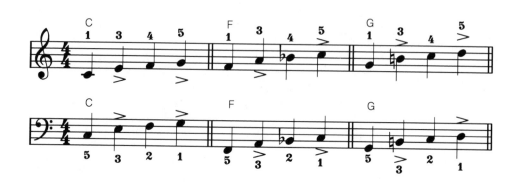

It is possible to combine these patterns. Following the twelve-bar blues progression on page 67, play one pattern with the right hand and the other with the left hand.

or

You can create an ensemble piece by combining patterns.

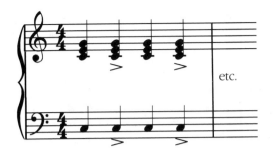

and

Creating Your Own Composition 4;
Writing a "Blues"

If you analyze the melody of "Blue Note Blues," you will discover that the pitches in each measure belong to the triad played by the left hand or that they are "blue notes" formed by flatting the third of the triad. You can improvise or write your own blues successfully in a similar manner. You create your melody by limiting the pitches to those found in the triad already assigned to each measure *plus* blue notes as you want to add them. The rhythm for the melody can be any that fits in the time signature given—usually $\frac{4}{4}$.

Here are a few combinations of pitches belonging to the C chord to get you started. You can probably come up with more interesting sequences of your own.

Once you find a sequence of pitches you like based on the C chord, you may want to use similar sequences based on the F and G chords when those chords occur in the progression. There is usually a bit of repetition in the melody of a twelve-bar blues.

Here is your basic chord progression. Fill in the treble staff with your own melody, or simply improvise a new melody each time you play the chord progression with the left hand.

_____ **BLUES**

(Your name)

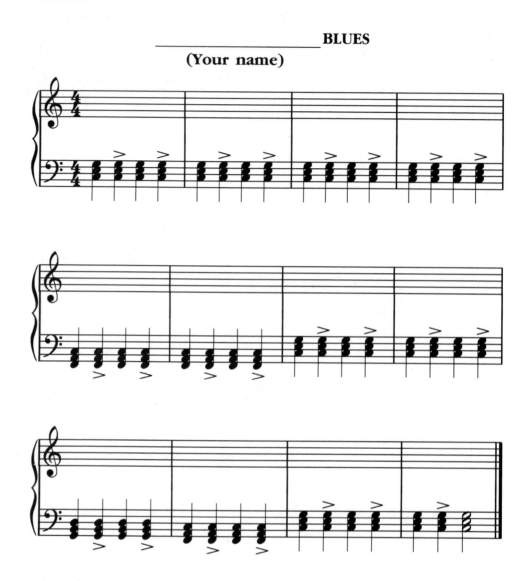

Theory Worksheet 5

A. Write the name of each interval in the blank below the staff.

_____ _____ _____ _____ _____ _____ _____ _____

B. Identify the following chords by their correct letter names.

_____ _____ _____ _____ _____ _____

C. Write the blue note belonging to each triad in the space provided.

D. Create four different measures of rhythmic notation for each time signature.

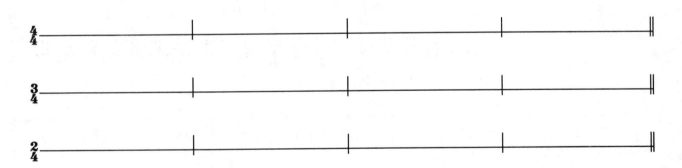

Chapter 7

Concepts	Skills
studies in touch	playing with different touches
the sound of minor	developing finger independence
	moving away from five-note melodies
	playing in the key of a minor

Studies in Touch

The development of different types of *touch* (the manner in which the keys are depressed) is necessary to the art of communicating the expressive qualities of piano music. The following series of exercises emphasizes *legato playing* (the smooth connection of consecutive pitches) and *staccato playing* (the detachment or separation of consecutive pitches).

Legato playing is indicated by curved lines, called *slur marks,* placed above or beneath the note heads of pitches to be played smoothly. Staccato playing is indicated by the placement of a dot, a *staccato mark,* above or beneath the head of each note to be played in a short, crisp manner.

In order to play the slurs in the first exercises, drop the wrist as you sound the first pitch and lift it as you play the final pitch. The last pitch in a slur should always be played softer than the others and should be sustained for slightly less than full value.

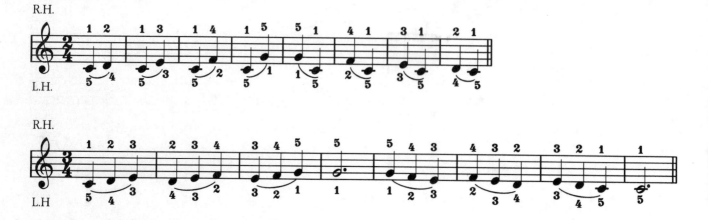

Staccato notes are to be played by throwing the hand and proper finger or fingers into the keys with a relaxed wrist. Staccato notes are not sustained for full value.

Playing with Different Touches

Once you become accustomed to the different touches involved in legato and staccato playing, you'll be able to attain a rich and varied sound when playing even the simplest of pieces. Experiment with legato and staccato in the following pieces.

FOLK DANCE

Allegretto*

Denmark

*Allegretto is a tempo marking indicating a speed slightly less lively than allegro.

GRANDMA SAYS

Allegro

U.S.

Here's another duet for you to practice.

SKATER'S WALTZ
(Excerpt)

Emil Waldteufel (1837–1915)
Arranged

Allegro grazioso*

*Grazioso is an Italian term indicating that the music should be played in a "graceful" manner.

Developing Finger Independence

Technical Exercise 3

This technical exercise is designed to help you increase your finger independence, develop greater speed of playing, and become accustomed to playing thirds between the first and second and the fourth and fifth fingers. Practice the exercise slowly with each hand alone, then with hands together. Gradually increase your tempo.

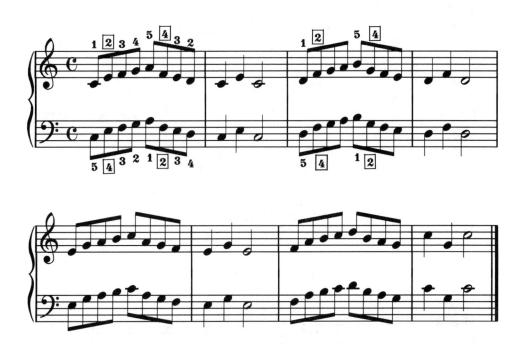

Rhythmic Exercises 5

These exercises are to be tapped, rapped, or played on pitches one octave apart.

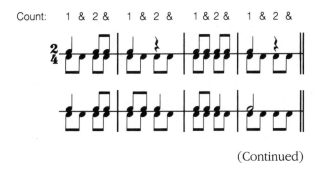

(Continued)

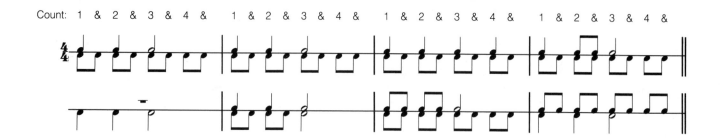

Moving Away from Five-Note Melodies

Notice the fingerings in this next composition. The third between F and A is played with R.H. fingers 1 and 2 and with L.H. fingers 3 and 4. Also, there are changes of fingers on repetitions of C in measures 2, 6, 10, and 14.

MARRE DE SI

Allegretto

Brazil

The interval of a third between E and G must be played with R.H. fingers 3 and 4 in this folk melody from Madagascar. Practice this stretch a few times before playing "Village Song."

■ **TO THE STUDENT:** *The left hand plays an ostinato containing fifths and sixths until the final measure.*

VILLAGE SONG

Andante

Madagascar

Watch the thirds that must be played by R.H. fingers 1 and 2 in this excerpt from a composition by Beethoven. Practice the third from F♯ to A until the thumb is accustomed to playing a black key.

GERMAN DANCE NO. 2
(Theme)

Allegretto grazioso

Ludwig van Beethoven
Arranged

dolce*

*Dolce is an Italian term meaning "sweet," usually used in music to imply that it should be performed at a soft dynamic level in a gentle manner.

The following Chippewa lullaby has an unusual feature: alternating $\frac{3}{4}$ and $\frac{2}{4}$ time signatures. The ♩ always receives the same amount of time, so the beat remains steady.

■ **TO THE STUDENT:** *The left-hand accompaniment consists of fifths and sixths.*

LULLABY

Andante

Chippewa

The Sound of Minor

Many musical compositions are based on sequences of pitches called *minor scales*. These scales have qualities much different from those of major scales. Listen to the following scales played by your instructor. One is major, the other minor, but the two begin and end on the same pitch.

The differences between the qualities (sounds) of major and minor are created by differences in the arrangements of intervals in each scale. The A minor scale just notated contains this sequence of whole steps and half steps: *whole, half, whole, whole, half, whole, whole.* In other words, the half steps are between steps 2 and 3 and steps 5 and 6. In major, the half steps fall between steps 3 and 4 and steps 7 and 8. Unlike major scales, which have only one pattern or form, minor scales can follow one of three patterns or forms. Here are examples of two of those three forms: *natural minor* and *harmonic minor.* The pattern of steps is indicated for each scale.

natural minor

harmonic minor

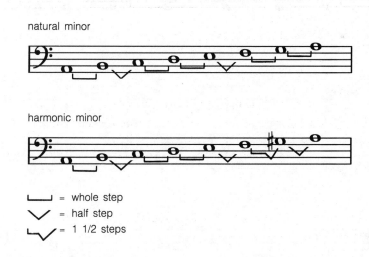

⌞__⌟ = whole step

∨ = half step

⌞∨ = 1 1/2 steps

Playing in the Key of A Minor

The key signature for pieces in A minor contains no sharps or flats, as with the key of C. Try out this folk melody and notice how different it sounds from the pieces you played before in the key of C.

FOLK MELODY

The following minuet by Händel includes new musical signs, *repeat signs*. The sign instructs the player to return to the beginning of a composition and play the selection again, or to return to the sign and play that section again. Notice that the end of the eighth measure contains both. After you play the first eight measures a second time, you play measures 9–16, then play those measures again.

■ **TO THE STUDENT:** *The left hand changes position in measure 9, then returns to its original position in measure 13.*

MINUET IN A MINOR

Georg Friedrich Händel
Arranged

The Japanese melody on the next page has been arranged as a duet for two pianos in the key of A minor.

SAKURA

Japan
Arranged

In addition to playing thirds between adjacent fingers in order to play melodies with an extended range, you must sometimes pass the thumb (first finger) underneath another finger to make a comfortable fingering possible. Practice this short exercise several times before playing the French carol "Pat-a-Pan."

PAT-A-PAN

Allegro

France

Creating Your Own Composition 5

This assignment involves writing a short composition in A minor. Your melody should be based on the pitches A, B, C, and E, with A as a final note. The rhythm, in $\frac{3}{4}$ time, should includes these notes: ♩, ♩, ♫. Your accompaniment could be based on one of the following *drones* (a drone is a pattern composed of two simultaneous pitches repeated over and over with little or no change) or ostinati—or an ostinato of your own based on several of these pitches: A, B, C, E, F.

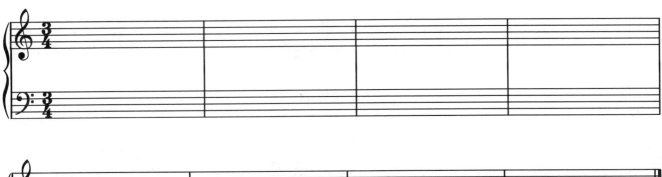

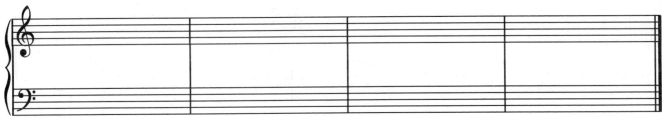

Theory Worksheet 6

A. Write the appropriate counting procedures above the notes in the following examples.

Count:

Count:

Count:

B. Identify the following scales by name and quality (for example, A major, D minor).

1. _____
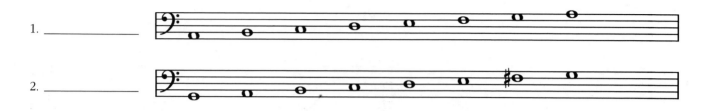

2. _____

C. Add a whole note to the right of each note given to form the interval indicated below the staff.

8va   prime   7th   3rd   5th   6th   4th   2nd

D. On each staff place two whole notes on lines and spaces whose letter names are given beneath, as the example indicates.

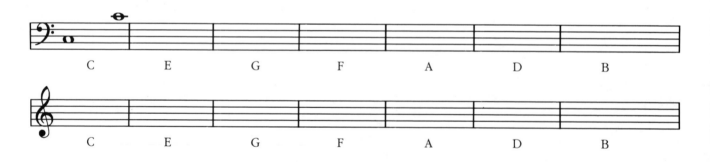

C   E   G   F   A   D   B

C   E   G   F   A   D   B

More Music to Read and Play

WILLIE

Moderato

U.S.

The melody of "Coventry Carol" contains G♯s to be played by crossing the second finger over the thumb of the right hand.

COVENTRY CAROL

Andante

England

*Watch the C♯! "Coventry Carol" ends with a major sound instead of minor.

More Music to Read and Play

Chapter 8

Concepts	Skills
key signatures	playing scales
major keys	accompaniment patterns
minor keys	using the damper pedal
key relationships	
tonic and dominant seventh chords	
lead sheet chord symbols	
a new time signature: $\frac{6}{8}$	

Playing Scales

In order to play the eight pitches of a major or a minor scale with one hand, you must not only be able to tuck your thumb smoothly under another finger, but also be able to bring another finger over the thumb to place your hand in a new position. The following exercises prepare you for this technique.

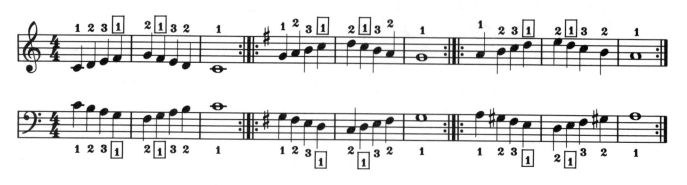

These scales are all played with the same fingering.

C MAJOR

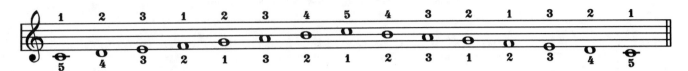

G MAJOR

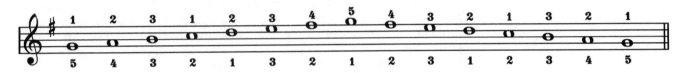

A MINOR

■ **TO THE STUDENT:** *All major and harmonic minor scales are in Appendix B with correct fingerings.*

Key Signatures

Any key on the keyboard can serve as the *tonic,* or first step, of both major and minor scales. These scales provide vocabularies of pitches used in musical compositions. Each scale is identified by a *key signature* located directly after the clef sign on the staff. Here is a guide to the interpretation of key signatures.

Major Keys

1. The absence of sharps or flats in a key signature identifies the key of C major.

2. When one or more sharps appear in a key signature, the sharp farthest to the right is always on the seventh step of the major scale. The next line or space above is the tonic.

3. One flat indicates the key of F major. When there are two or more flats, the flat second to the right is on the tonic.

Minor Keys

Each minor scale is represented by the key signature of a major scale. For instance, C major and A minor are both represented by the key signature containing neither sharps nor flats. Because they share a common key signature, A minor is called the *relative minor* of C major. The tonic of each minor scale is located three half steps below the tonic of its relative major scale.

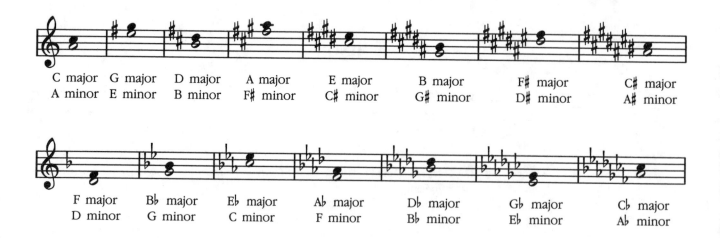

| C major | G major | D major | A major | E major | B major | F♯ major | C♯ major |
| A minor | E minor | B minor | F♯ minor | C♯ minor | G♯ minor | D♯ minor | A♯ minor |

| F major | B♭ major | E♭ major | A♭ major | D♭ major | G♭ major | C♭ major |
| D minor | G minor | C minor | F minor | B♭ minor | E♭ minor | A♭ minor |

Key Relationships

The following charts show the relationships among key signatures. Chart A shows the relationships among major key signatures. Chart B shows the relationships among minor key signatures. Notice that on Chart A, moving clockwise around the circle, the keys begin with C major and move from one to the next by the interval of a *perfect fifth* (an interval containing seven half steps). On Chart B, beginning with A minor, the keys move clockwise from one to the next also by the interval of the perfect fifth.

CHART A
The Circle of Fifths: Major Keys

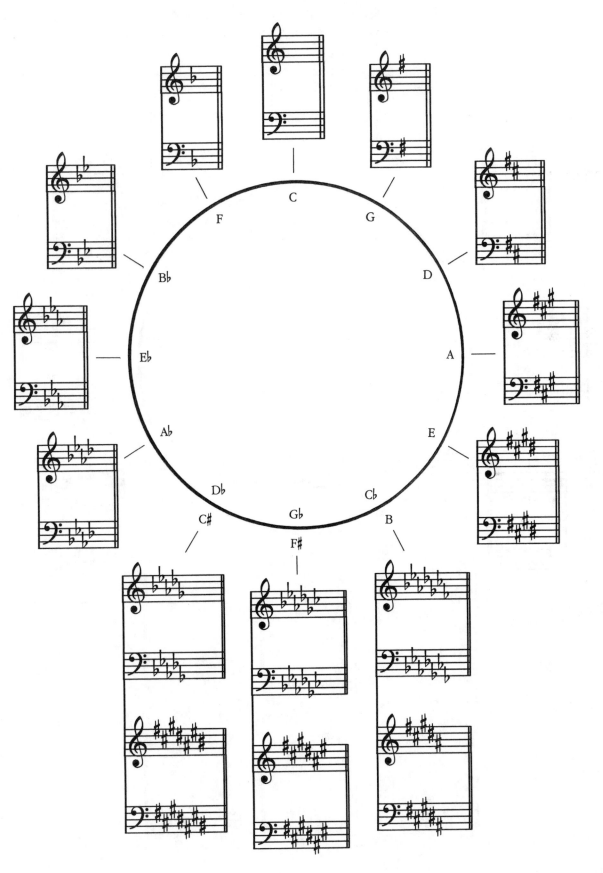

CHART B
Minor Key Signatures

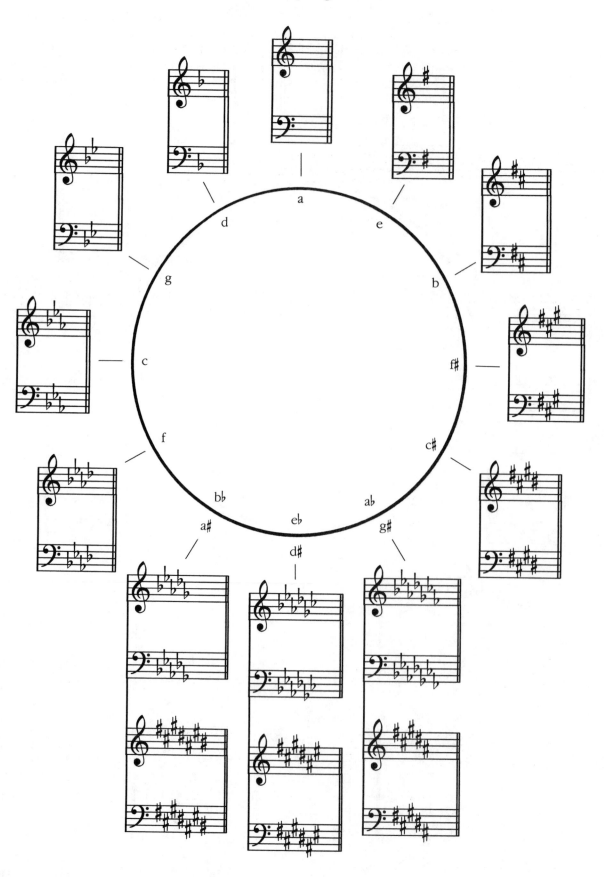

Tonic and Dominant Seventh Chords

In any major or minor scale, the first tone is called the *tonic*. The triad built with the tonic as its root is called the *tonic chord* or the *I chord*. The fifth tone in any major or minor scale is called the *dominant*. A chord for which the dominant is the root is called a *dominant chord* or a *V chord*. In the next examples, the dominant chord contains four tones and is called a *dominant seventh chord* or a *V7 chord*. The addition of the term *seventh* refers to the fact that the fourth tone is a seventh above the root of the chord.

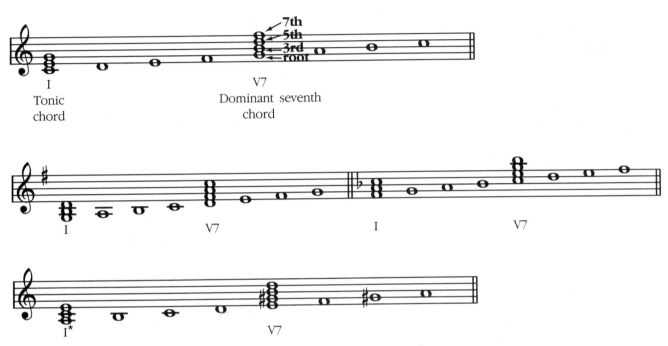

*The quality of the tonic chord in minor is minor. In a major triad there are four half steps between the root and the third. In a minor triad there are three half steps between the root and the third. Compare the sounds of major and minor triads containing the same root.

A smooth transition from the I chord to the V7 chord can be made if one of the tones of the V7 chord is omitted and the others are rearranged as in the following examples.

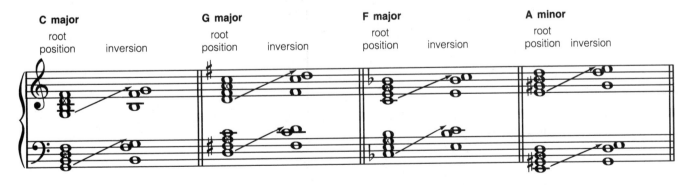

Notice that in each case the fifth of the chord is omitted and the root is moved to the top position in the chord.

Practice these next exercises until the chord changes can be played smoothly with each hand.

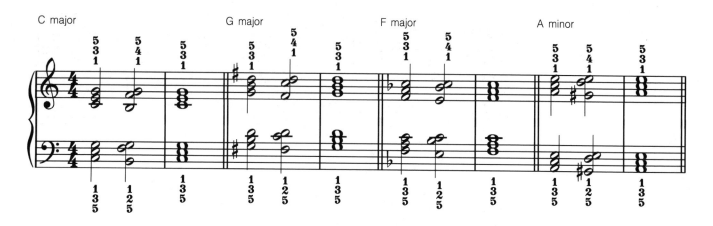

You will find many melodies with chordal accompaniments utilizing the V7 in its inversion throughout the rest of this book.

Here's a familiar melody in three major keys with chordal accompaniment.

DOWN IN THE VALLEY

Andante

U.S.

DOWN IN THE VALLEY

Andante

U.S.

DOWN IN THE VALLEY

U.S.

Now try this collection of pieces from various countries around the world. The first three are written in major keys: C, F, and G. The last one is in the key of A minor.

MARY AND MARTHA

CHIAPENECAS

DANCE MELODY

LOVE SONG

Accompaniment Patterns

Here are examples of accompaniment patterns that can be created using the three tones of the I and V7 chords. After you have practiced them, try utilizing them to accompany the previous melodies.

■ **TO THE STUDENT:** *Be sure to pick an accompaniment with the same meter as the melody.*

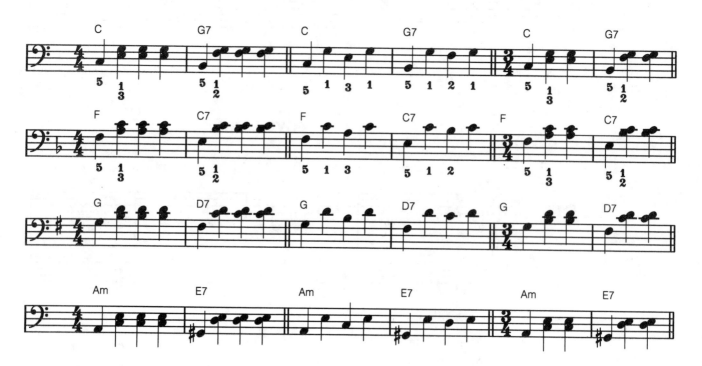

Lead Sheet Chord Symbols

Lead sheets for popular and folk music traditionally contain a notated melodic line with the appropriate chords to be used for accompaniment designated above the staff. Each chord is indicated by a capital letter representing its root and other symbols identifying its quality. The arabic number 7 represents the dominant seventh chord; the lowercase letter *m* or the letters *mi* are used to represent a minor triad.

The next melodies include chord symbols in lead sheet style. Practice them first with block chords for an accompaniment, then with accompaniment patterns suggested above.

ODE TO JOY
(Excerpt)

Ludwig van Beethoven (1770–1827)
Arranged

LOVE SOMEBODY

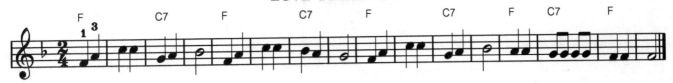

FAIS DO DO
(Excerpt)

France

WE THREE KINGS
(Excerpt)

Traditional

Rhythmic Exercises 6

These exercises are to be rapped, tapped, or played.

Count: 1 & 2 &   1 & 2 &   1 & 2 &   1 & 2 &

Count: 1 & 2 & 3 &   1 & 2 & 3 &   1 & 2 & 3 &   1 & 2 & 3 &

(Continued)

Count: 1 & 2 & 3 & 4 &   1 & 2 & 3 & 4 &   1 & 2 & 3 & 4 &   1 & 2 & 3 & 4 &

A New Time Signature: $\frac{6}{8}$

Familiarity with the $\frac{6}{8}$ time signature will open up a vast repertoire of compositions to play and enjoy. Try out the two rhythmic exercises below before you sight-read the next few pieces.

Rhythmic Exercises 7

Count: 1   2   3   4   5   6   1   2   3   4   5   6   1   2   3   4   5   6   1   2   3   4   5   6

Count: 1 & 2 & 3 & 4 & 5 & 6 &   1 & 2 & 3 & 4 & 5 & 6 &

Here are some compositions written in $\frac{6}{8}$ time. The first one will probably be familiar to you.

POP! GOES THE WEASEL

England

Analyze the intervals in the left-hand accompaniment of this dance from Turkey. Practice them carefully before adding the melody.

DANCE
(Excerpt)

Turkey

Now try this accompaniment pattern for $\frac{6}{8}$ time before you play "Pájara Pinta."

PÁJARA PINTA

Moderato

Latin America

*The thumbs of both hands share the white key D at the beginnings of each phrase from here to the end.

The following duet has been arranged for four hands at one piano.

POET AND PEASANT OVERTURE
(Excerpt)

Franz von Suppé (1819–1895)
Arranged

Using the Damper Pedal

The right pedal (the damper pedal) can be used to create a legato effect and an enriched sound. When the pedal is depressed, all the felt dampers are moved off the strings, allowing them to vibrate until it is released.

The damper pedal is operated by the right foot. In order to control it as smoothly as possible, the ball of the foot is placed on the pedal while the heel of the foot maintains firm contact with the floor. (*Note:* You should seat yourself on your piano bench in such a way that your right foot can be placed in this position comfortably.)

Pedaling instructions are generally printed below the bass clef in this manner:

Coordinating the foot with the hands requires careful listening. First you sound a note, or notes, and *immediately* depress the pedal. The pedal must be released *just before* the next note or notes sound, then depressed again *just after* they sound.

Here are some simple pedaling exercises for you to practice.

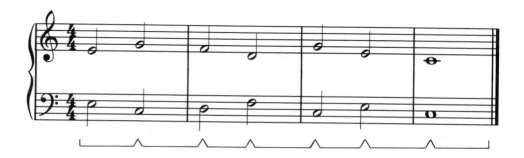

This well-known folk melody is presented to you here with pedaling marks indicated below the bass staff.

MICHAEL, ROW

U.S.

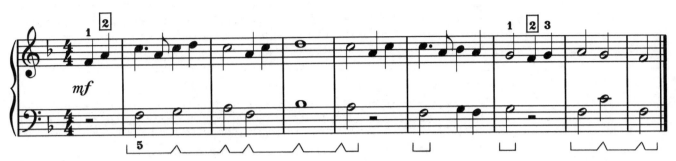

Creating Your Own Composition 6

An approach to composing a piece of music similar to that of creating a blues involves the following steps:

1. Establish a chord progression in which the tonic, or I, chord occurs both at the beginning and at the end. (In the key of C, the C chord will be the first and last chords.) Use the two chords with which you have been working, I and V7 (C and G7 in the key of C), assigning one chord per measure.

2. Choose a time signature and establish rhythm patterns for each measure. (A long note on the tonic in the final measure will create a sense of completion.)

3. Assign pitches from the appropriate chord to each note in your rhythm.

4. Create a left-hand accompaniment based on the chords in the chord progression. Be sure the rhythm fits the time signature you have selected.

Write your composition on the staves provided.

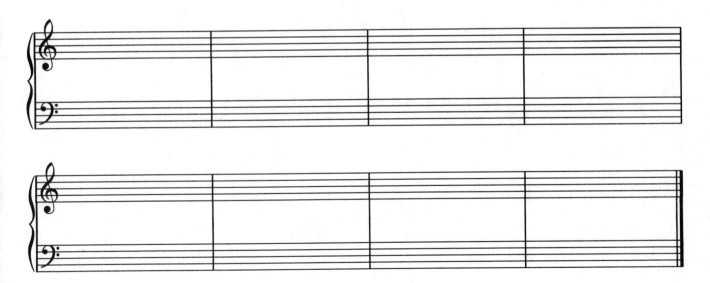

Theory Worksheet 7

A. Identify the major and relative minor keys represented by the following signatures.

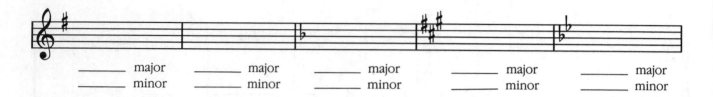

| _____ major | _____ major | _____ major | _____ major | _____ major |
| _____ minor | _____ minor | _____ minor | _____ minor | _____ minor |

B. Circle each chord that is in root position in the following series.

C. Fill in the blanks.

1. The first tone in any major or minor scale is called _____.

2. The fifth tone in any major or minor sale is called _____.

3. A complete seventh chord contains _____ tones.

4. The dominant in the key or scale of C is _____.

5. F is the tonic in the key or scale of _____.

D. Write the correct counting procedure above the notes in the following rhythm examples.

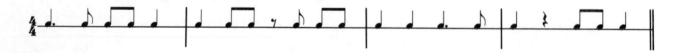

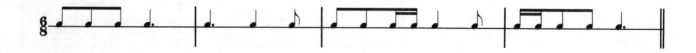

THE BIG CORRAL

Andante

U.S.

BARCAROLLE
(Theme)

Andante

Jacques Offenbach (1819–1880)

Chapter 9

Concepts	Skills
the subdominant chord	playing melodies with I, IV, and V7 accompaniments
syncopated rhythm	
passing tones	playing syncopated rhythms

The Subdominant Chord

The third of the three important chords for any key is the *subdominant chord,* or the *IV chord,* whose root is the fourth tone of a major or a minor scale.

The chord progressions you played on pages 66–67 included the subdominant chord in the key of C (the F chord) in its root position as you see it in the preceding example. The use of the three *primary* (important) triads—the tonic (I), the dominant (V), and the subdominant (IV)—in root position is traditional in blues style. A smoother transition from one chord to another can be made, however, if the tones of the subdominant chord are rearranged, or inverted.

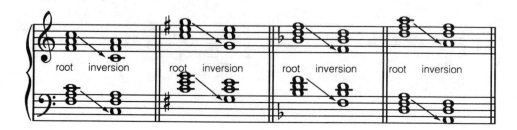

The next exercises will prepare you to use the subdominant chord in its inversion in accompaniments for folk and other simple melodies.

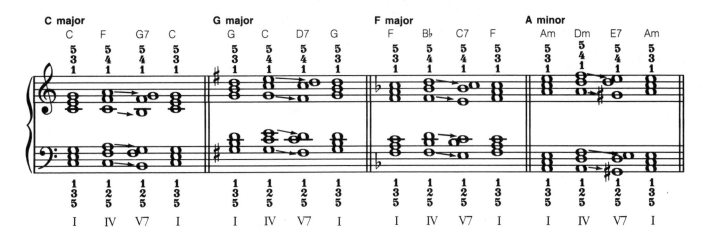

Here is a familiar melody in three major keys with chordal accompaniment.

WHEN THE SAINTS GO MARCHING IN

Key of C
Lively

U.S.

WHEN THE SAINTS GO MARCHING IN

Key of F
Lively

U.S.

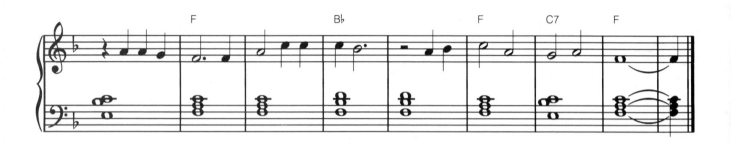

WHEN THE SAINTS GO MARCHING IN

Key of G
Lively

U.S.

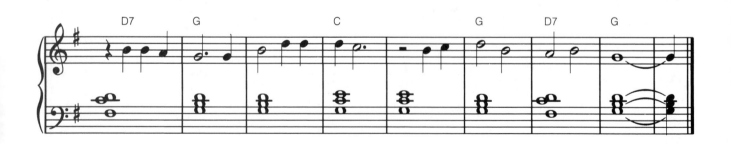

Playing Melodies with I, IV, and V7 Accompaniments

FOLK SONG

Nigeria

D.C. al Fine*

Moderato

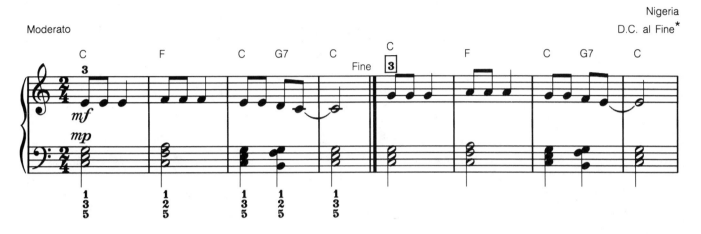

*D.C. al Fine (D.C. = Da Capo): Return to the beginning and play until you see the sign *Fine* (fée-nay), which means "the end."

ON TOP OF OLD SMOKY

Allegro

U.S.

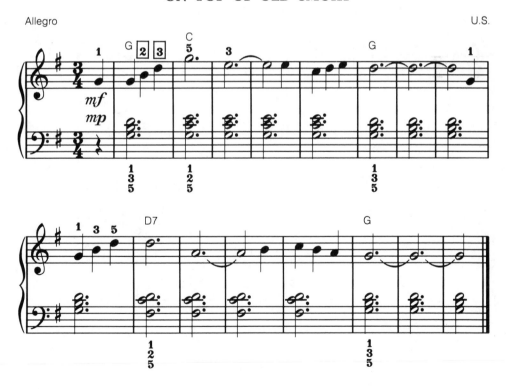

MARY HAD A BABY

Moderato

U.S.

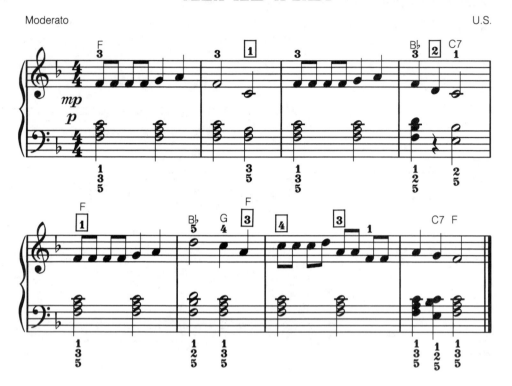

MY WHITE HORSE
("Mi Caballo Blanco")

Andante

Chile

112

Technical Exercise 4

This exercise will help you develop greater speed and independence of fingers. Practice it slowly at first, then increase your tempo. When you can play the exercise easily, try the next piece, "Tarantella."

TARANTELLA

Vivace is an Italian term indicating that the music is to be played at a quick, lively tempo.

Syncopated Rhythm

When we speak, certain syllables of words are normally accented or stressed more than others. When we make music, certain parts of measures are normally accented. The first beat of each measure is generally accented in all meters, and notes occurring *on* the beat generally receive more emphasis than notes occurring *after* the beat. When notes are arranged in such a way that a note of short value occurs *on* the beat and a note of long value occurs *after* the beat, or when *accent marks* indicate that emphasis is to be given to parts of a measure not normally accented (as in the case of most blues), *syncopation* occurs.

   Examples:

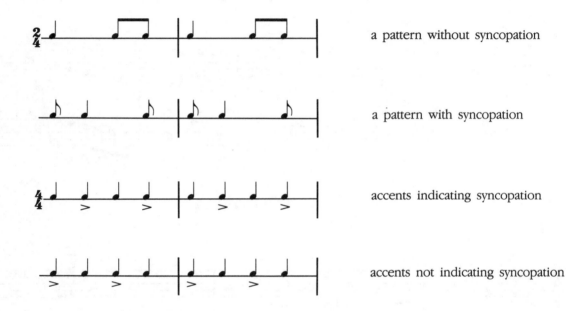

a pattern without syncopation

a pattern with syncopation

accents indicating syncopation

accents not indicating syncopation

Rhythmic Exercises 8

Count: 1 & 2 &   1 & 2 &   1 & 2 &   1 & 2 &

Playing Syncopated Rhythms

As you play the following composition, notice how the accented notes on traditionally unemphasized beats create the syncopated effect.

JOSHUA FOUGHT THE BATTLE

Where are the syncopated rhythms in this next composition?

RUSSIAN AIR

Allegretto

Russia

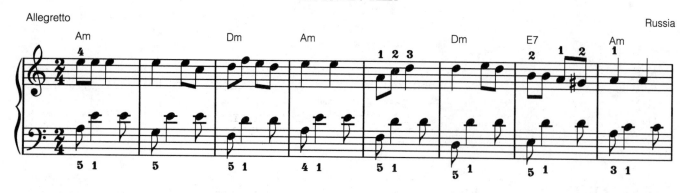

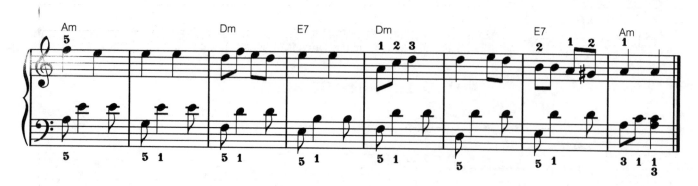

This rhythmic exercise will prepare you for the syncopated rhythms in the duet "In Bahia Town."

Count: 1 & 2 & 3 & 4 &   1 & 2 & 3 & 4 &   1 & 2 & 3 & 4 &   1 & 2 & 3 & 4 &

■ **TO THE STUDENT:** *Piano II plays an accompaniment based on the I, IV, and V7 chords.*

IN BAHIA TOWN

Try your hand at these accompaniment patterns in $\frac{4}{4}$, $\frac{3}{4}$, and $\frac{6}{8}$. The subdominant chord is presented in patterns previously suggested.

Now experiment with the following patterns in $\frac{6}{8}$ time.

Here's a folk melody in $\frac{6}{8}$.

EL TECOLOTE
("The Owl")

Allegretto

New Mexico

Lead Sheet Melodies

DRINK TO ME ONLY

Traditional

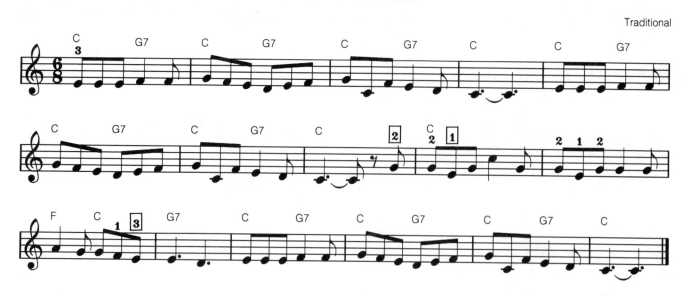

JACOB'S LADDER

U.S.

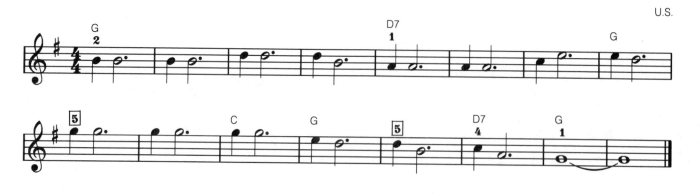

OPEN THE DOOR

Zulu

*Here are two endings for the second line. Play the first ending, make the repeat, play the second ending, then observe *D.C. al Fine.*

HATIKVAH

Israel

FOLK SONG

France

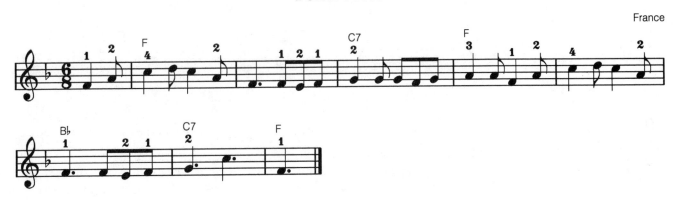

VENID PASTORES

Puerto Rico

Ve-nid pas - tor-es, ve - nid oh ve - nid a Be - lén oh ve - nid al por - tal, _____

Yo no me voy de Be - lén sin al ni - ño Je - sús in mo - men-to a-do - rar. _____

Creating Your Own Composition 7; Passing Tones

In Chapter 8 you discovered that once a chord progression is established, it is possible to create a melody by using pitches from the chords indicated in each measure. For instance, when the F chord is indicated, your melody might contain one or all of the pitches F–A–C. Sometimes you might wish to write or improvise a melody that moves by steps rather than one that skips from one chord tone to another. This can be done by adding *passing tones,* tones that pass between two chord tones.

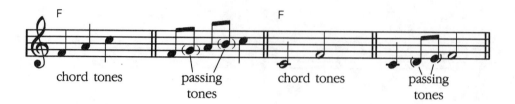

Another eight-measure chord progression is given here. As you create a melody, try to include some passing tones. Assign one of your standard accompaniment patterns to the left hand.

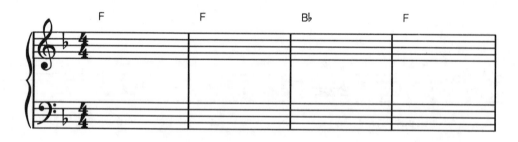

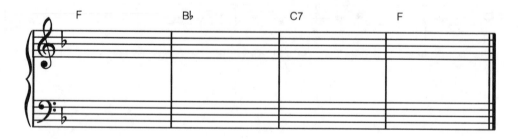

A.   Write the correct counting procedure above the notes and rests in each measure.

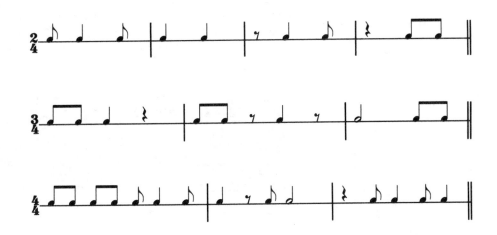

B.   Identify the following chords by their lead sheet symbols.

C.   Write the letter names of the pitches above each staff.

D.   Circle the measures that contain syncopated rhythms.

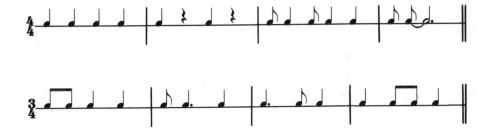

More Music to Read and Play

■ **TO THE STUDENT:** *Be sure to observe the accidentals in this next composition.*

GIVE ME YOUR HAND

Moderato

W. A. Mozart (1756–1791)

STREETS OF LAREDO

Andante

U.S.

Chapter 10

Concepts	Skills
a duet with syncopated rhythms	performing rhythms in $\frac{2}{4}$, $\frac{3}{4}$, and $\frac{4}{4}$ with sixteenth notes
a new key: d minor	playing in the Dorian mode
the Dorian mode	

A Duet with Syncopated Rhythms

In this duet for two pianos, Piano I plays syncopated rhythms created by tied eighth notes. Piano II plays a chordal accompaniment.

CIELITO LINDO

*The *fermata* (𝄐) is a symbol indicating that the note or notes under which
it is placed should be held longer than the usual time value.

Two selections by the twentieth-century Russian composer Dmitri Kabalevsky follow. Both hands play music written in the treble clef in "Polka." Which hand plays the melody? Note also the symbols that denote a change in volume. The *crescendo* sign, ◁, indicates that the music should become gradually louder. The *diminuendo*, or *decrescendo*, sign, ▷, indicates that the music should become gradually softer.

POLKA

Allegretto

Dmitri Kabalevsky (b. 1904)

A LITTLE DANCE

Allegro molto

Dmitri Kabalevsky

A New Key: D Minor

The next compositions are in the key of D minor, the relative minor of F major. Here is the scale of D minor, followed by its primary chords in both root and *inverted* (rearranged) positions. Notice that the fingering for the scale is the same as that for C major, G major, and A minor.

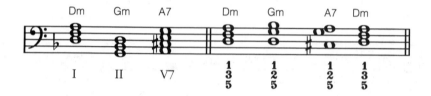

Earlier, you played "My White Horse" in the key of A minor. Here it is in D minor.

MY WHITE HORSE
("Mi Caballo Blanco")

Andante   Chile

Short Rhythm Exercise

Practice this exercise as preparation for the syncopated rhythmic patterns in "This Old Hammer."

THIS OLD HAMMER

U.S.

Heavily

This old ham-mer _ killed John Hen-ry. _ This old ham-mer _ killed John Hen-ry. _ This old

ham-mer _ killed John Hen-ry. _ It won't kill me, ____ it won't kill me.

Short Rhythm Exercise

This exercise will prepare you to play the rhythmic patterns in "Raisins and Almonds."

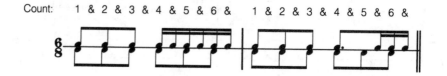

RAISINS AND ALMONDS

Moderato

Yiddish Folk Song

These two pieces will give you more practice playing dotted half notes, dotted quarter notes, and of course eighth notes. In "Masters in This Hall," concentrate on keeping your left and right hands together, particularly in the first and fifth measures.

FOLK DANCE

Allegro   Rumania

MASTERS IN THIS HALL

England

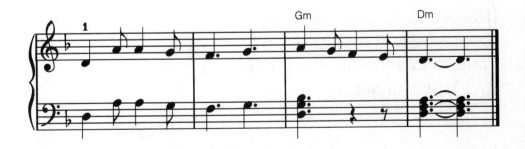

Now try this beautiful French carol with a partner.

CAROL

Andante   France

Performing Rhythms in $\frac{2}{4}$, $\frac{3}{4}$, and $\frac{4}{4}$ with Sixteenth Notes

To help you place sixteenth notes (notes receiving one fourth of a beat), use a counting procedure that breaks each beat into four equal parts. Here is one such method: 1 e & a 2 e & a, and so on. Practice this counting method in $\frac{2}{4}$, $\frac{3}{4}$, and $\frac{4}{4}$ time.

Rhythmic Exercises 9

These exercises are to be tapped or played.

Technical Exercise 5

Practice this exercise with a relaxed wrist. Let a rocking forearm movement help your fingers.

(THANKS TO CZERNY)

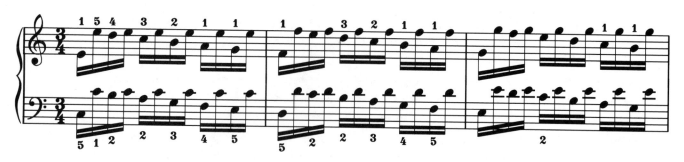

The Dorian Mode

In addition to pitch sequences and relationships that belong to major and minor scales and harmonic systems, there are a number of others, some of which are called *modes*. The next two compositions are in the *Dorian mode*. This mode is based on the following system of whole steps and half steps.

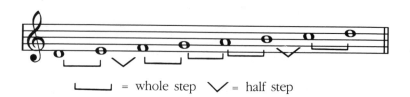

⌐_⌐ = whole step   ∨ = half step

Playing in the Dorian Mode

An excellent way to learn about and understand a particular mode is simply to listen—listen to the unique sounds a piece in a given mode will produce. Try these pieces, and listen carefully while you play.

DRUNKEN SAILOR

U.S.

SCARBOROUGH FAIR

Moderato

England

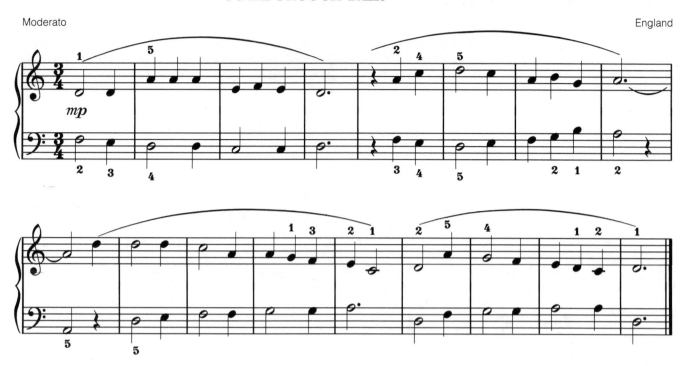

DANCE

Allegretto

Japan
Arranged

*Play this rhythm by rapping on a solid part of your keyboard instrument
or snapping your fingers.

More Experiences with Sixteenth Notes in $\frac{2}{4}$ and $\frac{3}{4}$

The more experience you have playing sixteenth notes the more comfortable you will be playing complex pieces. Try these two pieces, the first of which (an American folk melody) contains both rhythmic challenges and changing meter. Practice each hand separately first.

BARBARA ALLEN

SWEET POTATO

Creating Your Own Composition 8

An eight-measure chord progression is provided for a composition in D minor. Write a melody that utilizes chord tones and passing tones. Develop an accompaniment based on the assigned chords.

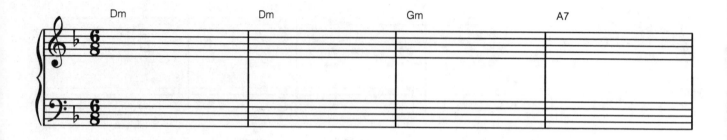

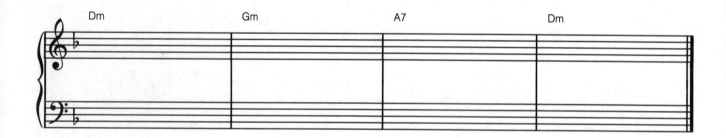

Theory Worksheet 9

A. Write the correct counting procedure above the notes and rests in the examples.

B. Write the series of pitches forming the Dorian mode that begins on C.

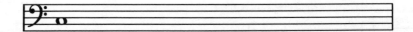

C. Circle the passing tones in the following melody.

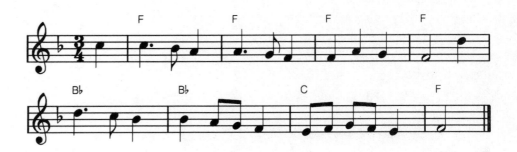

ROBIN ADAIR

Allegretto grazioso

Scotland

MELODY
(Mikrokosmos I)

Allegro

Béla Bartók (1881–1945)

CAPRICCIO

Franz Joseph Haydn (1732–1809)
Arranged

Moderato

MINUET

John Humphries (1707–1730)
Edited

Andante

*Watch the accidentals!

Chapter 11

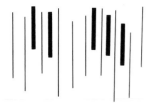

Concepts	Skills
the key of d major	playing in the key of d major
the key of b♭ major	playing music with more complex fingerings
	playing in the key of b♭ major

The Key of D Major

The scale of D major includes two sharps: F♯ and C♯. Practice the scale before proceeding. Notice that it has the same fingering as C major, G major, A minor, and D minor.

Playing in the Key of D Major

WHEN THE SAINTS GO MARCHING IN

U.S.

Lively

THE BANKS OF THE OHIO

Slowly

U.S.

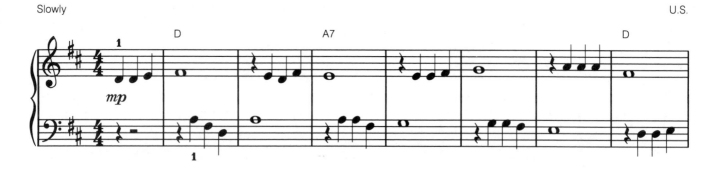

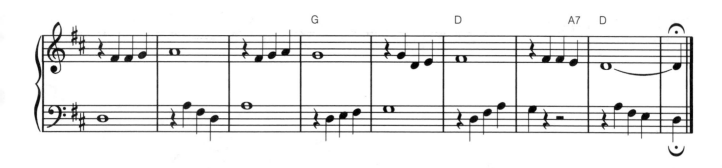

PALAPALA

Allegretto

Argentina

"The Lily," a duet for two persons at one piano, is based on a pentatonic scale in which the first pitch is D; thus, the key signature is that of D major. Pay particular attention to the clef signs at the beginning of each staff you are to play.

THE LILY

China
Arranged

■ **TO THE STUDENT:** *Additional accompaniments can be provided by creating ostinati based on the pitches D, E, F♯, A, B.*

Technical Exercise 6

Practice this exercise slowly at first, with a firm touch. As you increase your tempo, lighten your touch. Always practice with a relaxed wrist and a rocking forearm movement.

The primary chords in D major are D, G, and A7. Practice the progression based on these primary chords until you can play it smoothly.

I   IV   V7

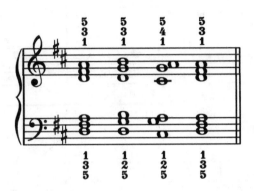

Here is "When the Saints Go Marching In" in D major with chordal accompaniment.

WHEN THE SAINTS GO MARCHING IN

Lively   U.S.

The following two pieces in D major contain different left-hand accompaniments.
Notice how the various accompaniment styles affect the general feeling of the music.

LAVENDER'S BLUE

Allegretto

U.S.

LA CALLE ANCHA
("The Broad Street")

Andante

Puerto Rico

Playing Music with More Complex Fingerings

Now try two more pieces written in D major, this time with slightly more complicated fingerings. Watch the sudden changes of the right-hand positions, for example in measures 3, 5, and 7 of the next composition.

MUSETTE
(Excerpt)

Johann Sebastian Bach (1685–1750)
From *A Notebook for Anna Magdalena Bach*

Allegro

DANCE

Moderato

Holland

The larger intervals contained in both the melody and the accompaniment of the "Emperor Waltz" excerpt require special practice, with careful attention given to their fingerings.

EMPEROR WALTZ
(Theme)

Johann Strauss, Jr. (1825–1899)
Arranged

Allegro

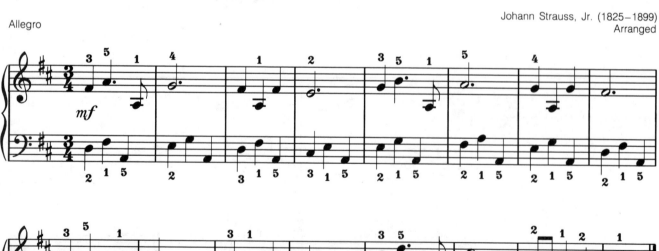

SONATA IN D, III
(Theme)

Allegro assai*

Franz Joseph Haydn (1732–1809)

*Assai is an Italian term meaning "very."

The Key of B♭ Major

The next compositions are in the key of B♭ major. The B♭ major scale includes two flats: B♭ and E♭.

Playing in the Key of B♭ Major

Use the next two songs to become accustomed to the sounds of B♭ major and to feel comfortable playing in two flats.

WHEN THE SAINTS GO MARCHING IN

Lively

U.S.

THE BANKS OF THE OHIO

Slowly

U.S.

The primary chords in B♭ major are B♭, E♭, and F7. Practice the progression based on the primary chords until you can play it smoothly.

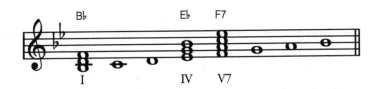

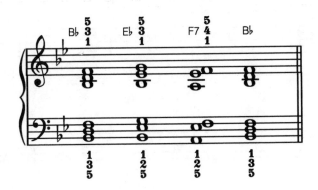

Here is a familiar melody in the new key of B♭ with chordal accompaniment.

JINGLE BELLS

U.S.

These last two pieces in B♭ offer two types of left-hand accompaniment. In the second piece, concentrate on playing the eighth notes evenly and steadily without breaking or pausing.

CAROL

Allegretto

Germany

HILITO DE ORO
("Golden Threads")

Moderato

Santo Domingo

Theory Worksheet 10

A. Create four contrasting measures of rhythmic patterns for each time signature.

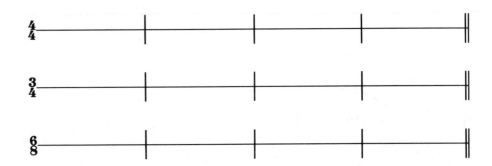

B. On each staff write the major scale represented by the key signature.

C. On each staff write the natural minor scale represented by the key signature.

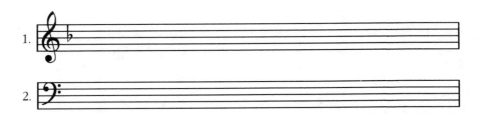

More Music to Read and Play

■ **TO THE STUDENT:** *Be sure to observe the accidentals in this next composition.*

NOCTURNE THEME
(*A Midsummer Night's Dream*)

Andante

Felix Mendelssohn (1809–1847)
Arranged

IN MAY

Allegretto

Germany

Chapter 12

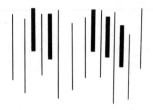

Concepts	Skills
lead sheet chord building	reading lead sheets
building triads	
building seventh chords	
building sixth chords	

Lead Sheet Chord Building

On page 98 you learned that collections of popular and folk music are often arranged in lead sheet form (including the melody, the words, and the chord symbols for each composition). For those of you interested in developing more advanced lead sheet reading and playing skills, an understanding of the basic elements of chord structure is essential. Acquisition of this understanding is facilitated by becoming familiar with the building blocks of our traditional harmonic system—the intervals called major and minor thirds (referred to briefly earlier in this text).

Major thirds are thirds encompassing four half steps—for instance, the distances from C to E and from G to B.

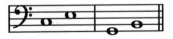

Minor thirds are thirds encompassing three half steps—for instance, the distances from E to G and from B to D.

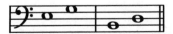

■ **TO THE STUDENT:** *All thirds look the same on the staff and must be checked aurally or visually at the keyboard to determine whether they are major or minor.*

Triads are three-toned chords whose pitches in root position are arranged in thirds. Four kinds of triads are possible: major, minor, augmented, and diminished.

Major triads include a major third and a minor third arranged in this manner:

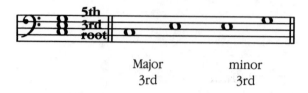

Minor triads include a major third and a minor third arranged in this manner:

Augmented triads include two major thirds:

Diminished triads include two minor thirds:

These are the lead sheet symbols used to designate the four kinds of triads. Remember that the letter name always labels the root of the chord.

Building Seventh Chords

Seventh chords are four-toned chords whose pitches in root position are arranged in thirds. Four kinds of seventh chords can be identified: dominant, major, minor, and diminished.

Dominant seventh chords include a major triad plus a second minor third arranged in this manner:

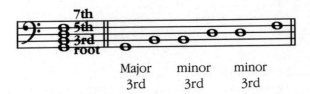

Major seventh chords include a major triad plus a second major third arranged in this manner:

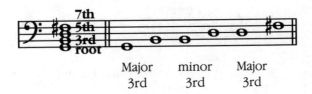

Minor seventh chords include a minor triad plus a second minor third arranged in this manner:

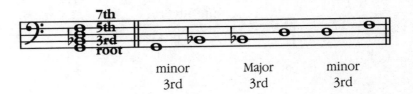

Diminished seventh chords include three minor thirds:

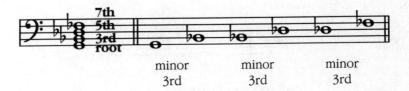

These are the lead sheet symbols used to designate the four kinds of seventh chords.

Building Sixth Chords

Some chords found in lead sheet arrangements belong to the family of sixth chords. Two kinds of sixth chords are most frequently used: major and minor.

Major sixth chords include a major triad plus a fourth pitch that is a sixth above the root of the chord. (This sixth is always a major second, or a whole step, above the fifth of the chord.)

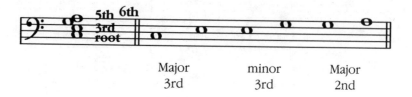

Minor sixth chords include a minor triad plus a fourth pitch that is a major second above the fifth of the chord.

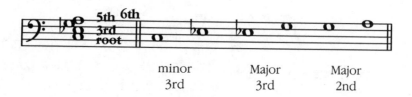

These are the lead sheet symbols used to designate the two kinds of sixth chords.

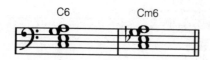

■ **TO THE STUDENT:** *You will find a chart of all the usual chords that occur in lead sheet music in Appendix A.*

A Collection of Popular and Folk-Style Compositions in Lead Sheet Arrangements

YESTERDAY

John Lennon (1940–1980)
Paul McCartney (b. 1942)

YOU'VE GOT TO HIDE YOUR LOVE AWAY

John Lennon
Paul McCartney

VICTORIA'S RAG

Lively

Victoria Williams (b. 1929)

AURA LEE

Not too fast

U.S.

As the black-bird in the spring, 'Neath the wil-low tree, _____

Sat and piped, I heard him sing, Sing-ing Aur-a Lee.

Aur - a Lee, Aur - a Lee, Maid with gold-en hair,

Sun-shine came a - long with thee, And swal-lows in the air.

THE WORRIED MAN BLUES

Steadily

U.S.

It takes a wor-ried man to sing a wor-ried song, It takes a wor-ried man to sing a wor-ried song, It takes a wor-ried man to sing a wor-ried song. I'm wor-ried now but I won't be wor-ried long._____

SINCE I LAID MY BURDEN DOWN

Rhythmically

U.S.

Glo - ry, glo - ry Hal-le - lu - jah! Since I laid my bur-den down. _ Glo - ry, glo - ry Hal-le - lu - jah! Since I laid my bur-den down. ____

CARELESS LOVE

Sadly

U.S.

Love, oh love, oh care-less love._____ Love, oh love, oh care-less love._____

Love, oh love, oh care-less love, can't you see what love has done to me?_____

THE RISIN' SUN

Slowly

U.S.

There is a house in New Or - leans, They call it the Ris - in'__ Sun._____

It's been the ru - in of man - y a soul And _ Lord knows I am one._____

Theory Worksheet 11

A. Using the notes given as the roots of chords, write the other notes that will complete the chords indicated by the symbols above the staff. (Add whole notes above the root.)

B. Write the appropriate counting procedures above the notes in each measure of the following examples.

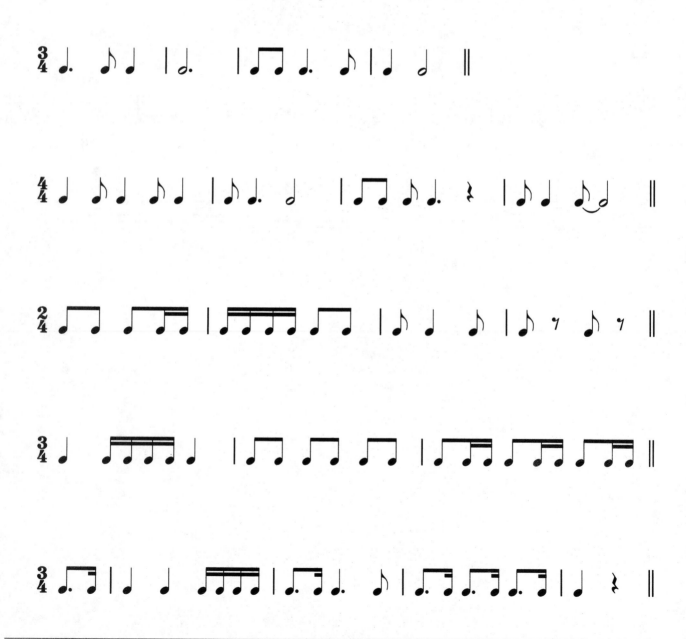

More Advanced Repertoire
Arranged in Chronological Order

MINUET IN G

Johann Krieger (1652–1735)
Edited

Andante

In "Tambourin" the left hand has to play a *grace note*, the small note ♪ . This D♯ is to be played as quickly as possible, leading into the half notes.

TAMBOURIN

Jean-Philippe Rameau (1683–1764)
Arranged

Allegro

THE TRUMPET

Allegro

Lord Byram (18th c.)

POLONAISE

Lively

Leopold Mozart (1719–1787)

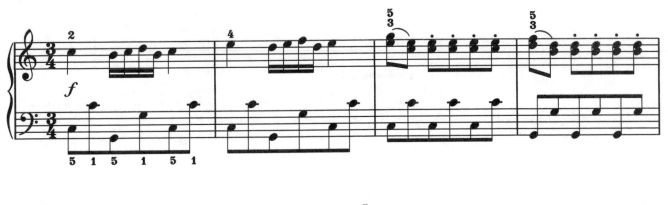

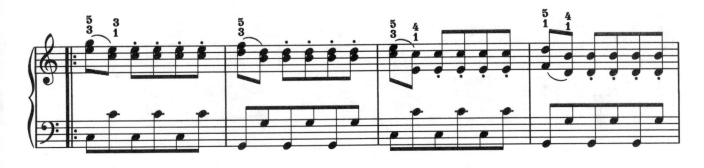

MINUET

Leopold Mozart
From *Notebook* for Wolfgang Amadeus, 1762 (edited)

Moderato

Fine

2nd time D.C. al Fine

SONATA
(Excerpt)

Franz Joseph Haydn (1732–1809)
Arranged

Tempo di Menuetto

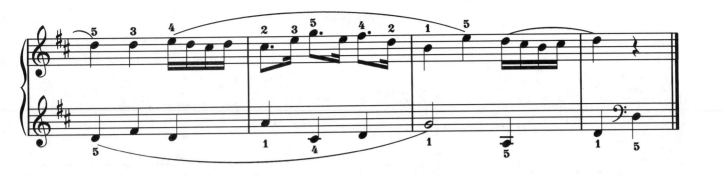

MINUET

Moderato

Wolfgang Amadeus Mozart (1756–1791)

DANCE

Allegro

Wolfgang Amadeus Mozart (1756–1791)

GERMAN DANCE

Lively

Franz Xavier Süssmayer (1766–1803)

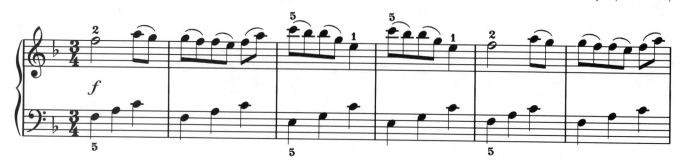

SONG WITHOUT WORDS
(Excerpt)

Felix Mendelssohn
Arranged

Presto*

Presto is an Italian term indicating a very fast tempo.

LITTLE PIECE

Moderato ♩=116*

Robert Schumann (1810–1856)

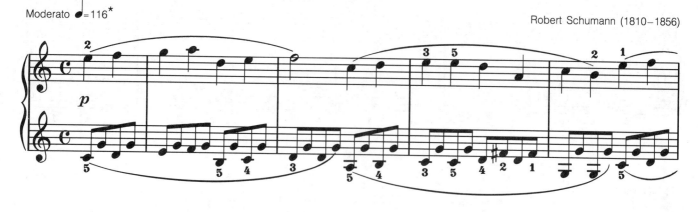

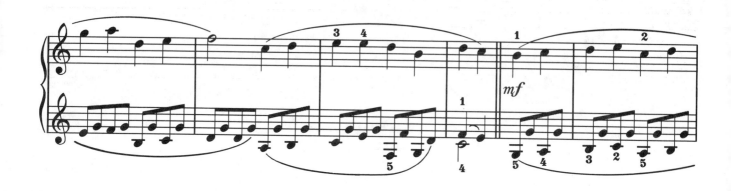

*♩=116 suggests that a metronome (a mechanical means of producing a sound on a steady beat) be set to sound 116 times per minute.

Here's a duet for two pianos.

ROSES FROM THE SOUTH

Johann Strauss, Jr.
Arranged

Liltingly

The next piece is a duet for four hands at one piano.

IN THE CITY OF THE CZAR'S DAUGHTER

Peter Illyich Tschaikovsky (1840–1893)
Arranged

Moderato

THE STRENUOUS LIFE
(Excerpt)

Not fast

Scott Joplin (1868–1917)

HUNGARIAN FOLK SONG

Allegretto

Béla Bartók (1881–1945)

LULLABY

Very gently ♩=76

Robert Gerster

STUDY

Allegro

Avrom Faderman (b. 1975)

Glossary of Musical Terms

Accent:	emphasis on a note or chord
Adagio:	slow tempo
Allegretto:	slightly less lively than allegro
Allegro:	lively tempo
Andante:	moderate, walking tempo
Andantino:	slightly quicker than andante
Animato:	animated
Con mòto:	with motion
Crescendo (cresc. or ————):	gradually increase loudness
Da capo (D.C.):	from the beginning
Diminuendo (dim. or ————):	gradually decrease loudness
Dolce:	sweetly
Fermata (⌢):	prolong a note or rest beyond normal value
Fine:	the end
Forte (*f*):	loud
Fortissimo (*ff*):	very loud
Legato:	smooth, connected playing
Lento:	very slowly
Mezzo forte (*mf*):	moderately loud
Mezzo piano (*mp*):	moderately soft
Moderato:	moderate speed
Ostinato:	a short melody repeated over and over
Pianissimo (*pp*):	very soft
Piano (*p*):	soft
Ritardando (rit.):	gradually getting slower
Sempre:	always
Staccato:	short detached playing
Vivace:	quick, lively

Lead Sheet Chord Chart

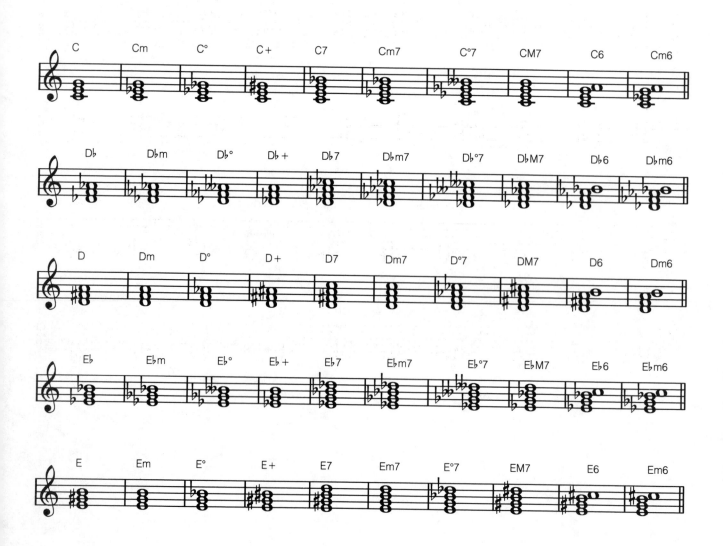

Appendix B

Major Scales and Fingerings

MAJOR SCALES AND FINGERINGS

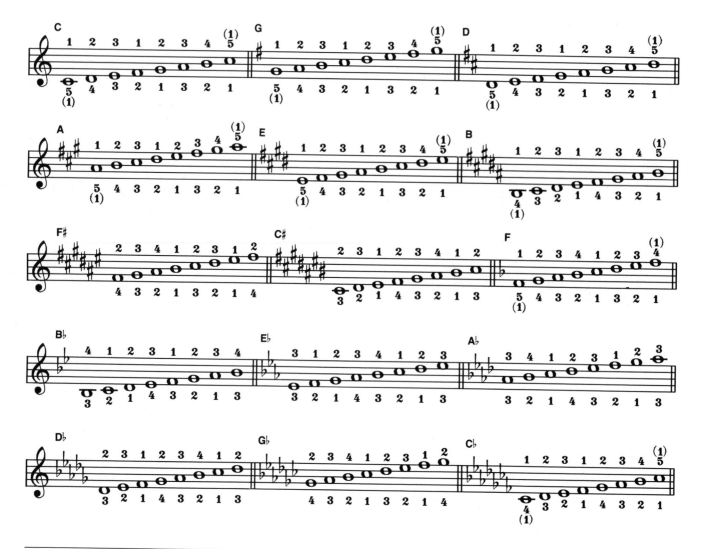

SELECTED HARMONIC MINOR SCALES AND FINGERINGS

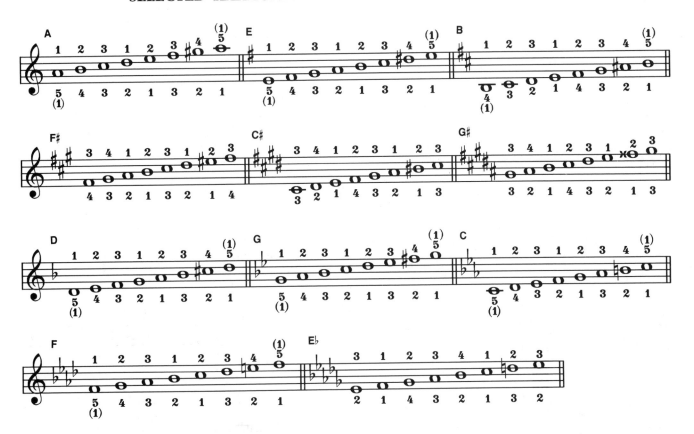

Index of Solo Compositions

Amazing Grace (U.S.), 12
At the Beginning (D.G. Türk), 33
Auld Lang Syne (Scotland), 12
Aura Lee (U.S.), 163
Banks of the Ohio, The (U.S.), 144, 152
Barbara Allen (U.S.), 137
Barcarolle (Offenbach), 107
Bee, The (Germany), 29
Big Corral, The (U.S.), 107
Blue Note Blues (P.A.I.), 68
Capriccio (Haydn), 141
Careless Love (U.S.), 165
Carol (Germany), 154
Catch (England), 23
Catch as Catch Canon (England), 34
Chiapenecas (Mexico), 96
Christmas Song (Germany), 53
Coventry Carol (England), 87
Cuckoo, The (Germany), 35
Dance (Holland), 150
Dance (Japan), 136
Dance (Mexico), 56
Dance (Mozart), 174
Dance (Turkey), 101
Dance Melody (Hungary), 97
Down in the Valley (U.S.), 94, 95
Drink to Me Only (England), 120
Drunken Sailor (U.S.), 135
Du, Du Liegst Mir im Herzen (Germany), 56
El Tecolote (New Mexico), 119
Emperor Waltz Theme (Strauss), 150
Fais Do Do (France), 99
Folk Dance (Denmark), 75
Folk Dance (France), 44
Folk Dance (Poland), 49
Folk Dance (Rumania), 131
Folk Melody (Russia), 82
Folk Song (France), 121
Folk Song (Nigeria), 111
German Dance (Süssmayer), 174
German Dance #2 (Beethoven), 80
Give Me Your Hand (Mozart), 124
Go from My Window (England), 61
Grandma Says (U.S.), 75
Hatikvah (Israel), 121
Hilito de Oro (Santo Domingo), 154
Hungarian Folk Song (Bartok), 183
In May (German), 156
In the Vineyard (Traditional), 52
Jacob's Ladder (U.S.), 120
Jingle Bells (Traditional), 21, 31, 41, 51, 53
Joshua Fought the Battle (U.S.), 115
La Calle Ancha (Puerto Rico), 148
Lavendar's Blue (U.S.), 23, 50

Lightly Row (German), 23, 50
Little Dance, A (Kabalevsky), 127
Little Piece (Schumann), 176
Love Song (North Africa), 97
Lullaby (Chippewa), 80
Lullaby (Gerster), 184
Lullaby (Wales), 8, 9
Mama Don't 'Low (U.S.), 11
Mandandiran (Chile), 36
March (Finland), 34
Marre de Si (Brazil) 78
Mary and Martha (U.S.), 96
Mary Had a Baby (U.S.), 112
Masters in This Hall (England), 131
Melody (Bartok), 140
Melody (Germany), 22, 28
Merrily We Roll Along (traditional), 8
Michael, Row (U.S.), 105
Minuet (Humphries), 142
Minuet (L. Mozart), 172
Minuet (W. A. Mozart), 173
Minuet in A Minor (Händel), 82
Minuet in C (Händel), 61
Minuet in G (Krieger), 168
Mostly Fifths, 24
Mostly Fourths, 24
Musette (Bach), 149
My Dove (Czechoslovakia), 34
My Lord! What a Morning (U.S.), 49
My White Horse (Chile), 112, 128
Nocturne (Mendelssohn), 156
Ode to Joy (Beethoven), 33, 40, 98
Old MacDonald (U.S.), 11, 31
On Top of Old Smoky (U.S.), 111
Open the Door (Zulu), 120
Pájara Pinta (Latin America), 102
Palapala (Argentina), 144
Pat-a-Pan (France), 84
Polka (Kabalevsky), 127
Polonaise (L. Mozart), 171
Pop! Goes the Weasel (England), 101
Quicker, Quicker! Round and Round (Türk), 43
Raisins and Almonds (Yiddish), 130
Risin' Sun, The (U.S.), 165
Robin Adair (Scotland), 140
Russian Air (Russia), 116
Scarborough Fair (England), 136
Shepherds' Hey (England), 48
Since I Laid My Burden Down (U.S.), 164
Sonata [Theme] (Haydn), 172
Sonata in D [Theme] (Haydn), 151
Song without Words [Theme]
    (Mendelssohn), 175

Index of Solo Compositions (continued)

Streets of Laredo (U.S.), 124
Strenuous Life, The (Joplin), 182
Study (Faderman), 186
Sweet Potato (U.S.), 137
Swing Low, Sweet Chariot (U.S.), 13
Tambourin (Rameau), 169
Tarantella (unknown), 113
Theme from Symphony #2 (Brahms), 33
This Old Hammer (U.S.), 129
Three Sons (U.S.), 45
Triads to Try (P.A.I.), 66
Trumpet, The (Lord Byram), 170
Turkey in the Straw (U.S.), 44

Venid Pastores (Puerto Rico, 121
Victoria's Rag (Williams), 163
Village Song (Madagascar), 79
Westminster Chimes (England), 30
We Three Kings (Traditional), 99
When the Saints Go Marching In (U.S.), 41, 52, 109, 110, 143, 147, 152
Willie (U.S.), 87
Worried Man Blues, 87
Worried Man Blues, The (U.S.), 164
Yesterday (Lennon & McCartney), 161
You've Got to Hid Your Love Away (Lennon & McCartney), 162

Index of Duets

Carol (France), 132
Cielito Lindo (Mexico), 125
Fais Do Do (France), 58
Fen Yang (China), 55
In Bahia Town (Brazil), 117
In the City of the Czar's Daughter (Tschaikovsky), 180
Jingle Bells (U.S.), 31

Lily, The (China), 145
Love Somebody (U.S.), 46
Poet and Peasant Overture [Theme] (von Suppe), 103
Roses from the South (Strauss), 178
Sakura (Japan), 83
Skater's Waltz Theme (Waldteufel), 76
Westminster Chimes (England), 30

CLASSIFIED INDEX

Melodies with Chord Symbols Given

Two-Chord Melodies

Barcarolle, 107
Bee, The 29
Big Corral, The, 107
Carol (Germany), 154
Chiapenecas, 96
Christmas Song, 53
Cuckoo, The, 35
Dance (Holland), 150
Dance Melody, 97
Down in the Valley, 94, 95
Drunken Sailor (Dm–C), 135
Fais Do Do, 99
Folk Dance (Denmark), 75
Grandma Says, 75
La Calle Ancha, 148
Lightly Row, 23
Love Somebody, 99
Love Song, 97
Mary and Martha, 96
Masters in this Hall, 131
Melody (Germany), 22, 28
My Dove, 34
Ode to Joy, 33, 98
Pájara Pinta, 102
Pop! Goes the Weasel, 101
Sweet Potato, 137
We Three Kings, 99

Three-Chord Melodies

Banks of the Ohio, The, 144, 152
Blue Note Blues, 68
Carol (Germany), 154
Drink to Me Only, 120
El Tecolote, 119

Folk Dance (France), 121
Folk Dance (Rumania), 131
Folk Song (France), 44
Folk Song (Nigeria), 111
Hatikvah, 121
Hilito de Oro, 154
Jacob's Ladder, 120
Jingle Bells, 21, 153
Joshua Fought the Battle, 115
Lavender's Blue, 148
Mary Had a Baby, 112
My White Horse, 112, 128
Old MacDonald, 31
On Top of Old Smoky, 111
Open the Door, 120
Raisins and Almonds, 130
Russian Air, 116
Streets of Laredo, 124
Tarentella, 113
This Old Hammer, 129
Venid Pastores, 121
When the Saints Go Marching In, 41, 52, 109,
      110, 147, 152
Willie, 87

Melodies with More than Three Chords

Aura Lee, 163
Careless Love, 165
Risin' Sun, The, 165
Since I Laid My Burden Down, 164
Victoria's Rag, 163
Worried Man Blues, The, 164
Yesterday, 161
You've Got to Hide Your Love Away, 162

Exercises, Worksheets, Activities

Chord progressions I-V7-I, 94
Chord progressions I-IV-V7-I, 109
Creative activities (Creating Your Own Composition), 36, 48, 58, 71, 84, 105, 122, 138
Damper pedal exercises, 105
Rhythmic exercises (major), 16, 27, 42, 53, 77, 99, 100, 114, 133

Rhythmic exercises (other), 116, 129, 130
Scale preparation, 88
Studies in touch, 74
Technical exercises, 57, 63, 77, 113, 134, 146
Theory worksheets, 24, 37, 47, 59, 73, 85, 106, 123, 139, 155, 166

Compositions by Known Composers

At the Beginning (Türk), 33
Barcarolle (Offenbach), 107
Capriccio (Haydn), 141
Emperor Waltz (Strauss), 150
German Dance #2 (Beethoven), 80
German Dance (Süssmayer), 174
Give Me Your Hand (W. A. Mozart), 124
Hungarian Folk Song (Bartok), 183
In the City of the Czar's Daughter (Tschaikovsky), 180
Little Piece (Schumann), 176
Little Dance, A (Kabalevsky), 127
Lullaby (Gerster), 184
Melody (Bartok), 140
Minuet (Humphries), 142
Minuet (L. Mozart), 172
Minuet (W. A. Mozart), 173
Minuet in A Minor (Händel), 82
Minuet in C (Händel), 61
Minuet in G (Krieger), 168
Musette (Bach), 149
Nocturne (Mendelssohn), 156

Ode to Joy (Beethoven), 33, 40, 98
Poet and Peasant Overture (von Suppe), 103
Polka (Kabalevsky), 127
Polonaise (L. Mozart), 171
Quicker, Quicker! Round and Round (Türk), 43
Roses from the South (Strauss), 178
Skater's Waltz Theme (Waldteufel), 76
Sonata Theme (Haydn), 172
Sonata in D Theme (Haydn), 151
Song without Words Theme (Mendelssohn), 175
Strenuous Life, The (Joplin), 182
Study (Faderman), 186
Tambourin (Rameau), 169
Theme from Symphony #2 (Brahms), 33
Trumpet, The (Lord Byram), 170
Victoria's Rag (Williams), 163
Yesterday (Lennon & McCartney), 161
You've Got to Hide Your Love Away (Lennon & McCartney), 162

SUBJECT INDEX

Accents, 66
   normal accents, 66
   syncopated accents, 66
Accidentals, 39
Accompaniment patterns, 70, 98, 118
Bar lines (defined), 14, 20
Beat (defined), 3
Blues, 66, 67, 68, 70
   accompaniment patterns, 70
   blue notes, 68
   progression, 67
Chords, 62, 64, 93, 108, 109, 127, 147, 153,
     157–160
   C chord, 62
   dominant seventh (V7), 93
   F chord, 64
   G chord, 64
   I, IV, V7 chords
     a minor, 109
     B-flat major, 153
     C major, 109
     D major, 147
     d minor, 128
     F major, 109
     G major, 109
   progressions, 66, 67
     twelve-bar blues, 66, 67
   seventh chords, 93, 159
     diminished, 159
     dominant, 93, 159
     major, 159
     minor, 159
   sixth chords, 160
     major, 160
     minor, 160
   subdominant (IV), 108, 109
   triads, 62, 158
     augmented, 158
     diminished, 158
     major, 158
     minor, 158
Circle of fifths, 91, 92
   major keys, 91
   minor keys, 92
Clefs, 17
Damper pedal use, 104
Dorian mode, 134–136
Dynamics, 20, 30, 127
   forte, 20

mezzo forte, 20
mezzo piano, 30
piano, 20
crescendo ⟨ , 127
decrescendo ⟩ , 127
diminuendo, 127
Enharmonic equivalents, 39
Fermata, 126
Flat sign, 38
Grace note, 169
Grand staff, 18
Grazioso, 76
Hand position, 2
Harmony (defined), 8
Improvisation, 42, 65, 67
Intervals, 22, 23, 24, 38, 69, 157
   fifths, 23, 24
   fourths, 23, 24
   half steps, 38
   seconds, 22
   sevenths, 69
   sixths, 69
   thirds, 22, 157
     major thirds, 157
     minor thirds, 157
   whole steps, 39
Key signatures, 40, 89, 90, 91
Lead sheet music (symbols and playing), 98,
     99, 120, 121, 157–160, 161–165
   lead sheet chord building, 157–160
   lead sheet chord symbols, 98
   lead sheet melodies, 98, 99, 120, 121,
     161–165
Legato, 5, 74
Measure (defined), 14
Melody (defined), 5
Meter (defined), 14
Metronome marking (defined), 176
Ostinato (defined), 9
   examples, 10, 55, 59, 79, 83, 107
Passing tones (defined), 122
Piano (the instrument), 1–2
Repeat signs, 82
Rhythm (defined), 3
Rhythmic notation (introduction), 14–15
Rhythmic patterns (defined), 14
Scales, 38, 39, 40, 50, 54, 81, 88, 89, 128, 143,
     151
   chromatic, 38

major (introduction), 39, 40
   b-flat major, 151
   c major, 39
   d major, 143
   f major, 40
   g major, 50
minor (introduction), 81
   a minor, 81
   d minor, 128
pentatonic, 54
playing scales, 88, 89
Sharp sign, 39
Sight reading, 22
Staff (defined), 17
Syncopation, 66, 114, 115, 116, 125, 129
Table of notes and rests, 15
Tempo (defined), 10
   markings (defined), 10, 22, 23, 29, 75, 151, 174
      allegretto, 75
      allegro, 23
      allegro assai, 151
      moderato, 22
      presto, 174
Tie (defined), 45
Time signatures, 16, 28, 80, 100, 137
   alternating time signatures, 80, 137
frequently used time signatures with explanations
   $\frac{2}{4}$, 16
   $\frac{3}{4}$, 16
   $\frac{4}{4}$, 16
   $\frac{2}{2}$, 16
   $\frac{6}{8}$, 16, 100
   C, 18
Touch (playing approaches), 5, 74, 75
   legato, 5, 74
   slurs, 74
   staccato, 74, 75
Transposing, 51, 56